RE-MADE
IN THE USA

HOW WE CAN **RESTORE JOBS**, **RETOOL MANUFACTURING**, AND **COMPETE WITH THE WORLD**

TODD LIPSCOMB

WILEY

John Wiley & Sons, Inc.

Published by John Wiley & Sons, Inc., Hoboken, New Jersey.
Published simultaneously in Canada.

For general information on our other products and services or for technical support, please contact our Customer Care Department within the United States at (800) 762-2974, outside the United States at (317) 572-3993 or fax (317) 572-4002.

Wiley also publishes its books in a variety of electronic formats. Some content that appears in print may not be available in electronic books. For more information about Wiley products, visit our web site at www.wiley.com.

Library of Congress Cataloging-in-Publication Data:

Lipscomb, Todd, 1966–
    Re-made in the USA : how we can restore jobs, retool manufacturing, and compete with the world / Todd Lipscomb.
        p. cm.
    Includes index.
    ISBN 978-0-470-92992-6 (cloth)
    ISBN 978-1-118-02581-9 (ebk)
    ISBN 978-1-118-02582-6 (ebk)
    ISBN 978-1-118-02583-3 (ebk)
        1. United States—Economic conditions—21st century. 2. United States—Social policy—21st century. 3. Labor market—United States. 4. Industrial policy—United States. 5. International trade. I. Title.
    HC106.84.L57   2011
    330.973—dc22

                                                                    2010045232

Printed in the United States of America

10 9 8 7 6 5 4 3 2 1

For my dear wife Kaori, daughter Lyndsey, and son Lance.
You taught me the real meaning of joy.

Contents

Introduction

Just a few short decades ago, our country led the world in manufacturing and politics. In those few intervening years, the tide has turned. We've largely lost our manufacturing base and seen the twilight of our political leadership. At first glance, those concepts might seem far removed from the average American's life. It's sad, of course, to see a strong and innovative country like the United States decline, but it's very easy to get caught up in the day-to-day details of living our own lives and think of global issues as simply too big, too distant, to be our primary focus. In fact, there is no distinction. The future of the United States is our future. Manufacturing and political influence are inextricably intertwined with that future, and with the solid middle-class jobs manufacturing provides.

Today, we stand at a crossroads, called to choose between renewal and stagnation. Yes, today's circumstances are dire and discouraging. We're surrounded by economic decay and all that stems from it. But make no mistake: We have a choice. There is hope, if we believe. There is hope, if we are willing to act.

Living and working in Asia for more than seven years gave me some disturbing insights into America's place in the global market. The imbalance in the present trade situation is ominous; every other nation I've observed or studied puts its own interests first. Only in the United States are we handicapped by the rules of "free trade." That we deem such a vague concept as more important than our own factories and people is a joke abroad. The lessons I learned in my years in Asia, and what they mean to the USA, haunt me to this day.

Those lessons inspired me to found MadeinUSAForever.com, which has grown into a significant resource for those interested in buying products made in the USA. But I wanted to do more with the information and motivation I'd gathered overseas. I started the company in 2007 with a handful of suppliers for the purpose of creating options for those who want to buy American. The response has been beyond my wildest expectations. We now have thousands of products and tens of thousands of customers.

I am often asked why an expert on Asia would go to all this effort for the USA. Was there a single reason? Some sort of epiphany? A moment of realization? It was more like a dozen or more reasons and ideas coming together over time. One defining moment came when I held my newborn daughter in my arms for the first time and realized what this country's decline would cost her and her generation if we didn't take action now.

My education and background are in finance, although I have always had a love of history. I have read hundreds of history and cultural books, and leapt at the chance to live in Asia, twice. Living in Asia broadened my knowledge base tremendously and gave me a great deal of real-world experience abroad. As my knowledge grew, it became disconcerting as I watched American coworkers come to Asia, spend a few nights at the Hilton, and return home as "experts." It was important to me to get out among the people and familiarize myself with the history and culture of each locale and country. The lessons I learned related not just to what I was seeing, but to our own people and our great nation, as well.

Global relationships have changed dramatically over the past several decades. No nation or population is isolated today. And few individuals have enough information to truly understand the complex web of connections and influences. Those currently in power positions in business and government are often well served by keeping that information under wraps. Ten years ago, I still believed what I had learned in college about America and our place in the world: "Free trade" was innately fair, and if we had a problem here, it must be because wages were too high. That view proved to be far too simplistic. I have seen firsthand that we are the only major nation with its doors wide open to imports. Efforts to export to any other major nation are met with countless obstacles. Why? Because every other nation takes care of its own interests first.

Many in Washington and Asian capitals realize the United States is too open and that the trade imbalance has created a grotesque, unsustainable situation. Cheap goods are exported to this country in exchange for currency that is then loaned back to the United States, perpetuating the system. Asia gets the factories and the future. We get cheap goods today and a dire future. Yet nothing is done about it.

Sadly, many American businesspeople not only ignore the problems, but encourage them. Procurement officials for major chain stores send drawings, designs, and other information about items produced by their American suppliers abroad, in search of lower and lower prices. Previous generations of retailers, bankers, and corporate executives remembered that they were Americans first, and were conscious of, and took responsibility for, the impact of their choices on our national economy. Today, it seems that many remember that they are Americans only when they need a bailout. This ultrashort-term view values a penny in cost over keeping an American factory down the street in business. It also encourages lower-quality imports. Planned obsolescence keeps the cycle going, and encourages Americans to send more and more dollars overseas.

Put it all together and we see the true cost of this model in American unemployment, falling real wages, and massive debt—and those are just the economic factors. We're also feeding a lack of worker safety, product safety, and pollution controls in these foreign factories. The end result is a model in which we get chintzy, throwaway products at cheaper and cheaper prices. To shoppers seeing lower prices at the register, it might seem beneficial, but this trade and debt imbalance is not mathematically sustainable on any level in the years to come. Ultimately, we will all pay a hefty price for those few pennies saved today.

If it sounds like I'm biased in favor of the USA, it's because I am. After many years of studying history and foreign cultures, I strongly believe that there are unique, special things about this country that must be preserved. We take it for granted today, but freedom and democracy are actually very rare exceptions to the rule in history. Even today, billions of people live in tyrannical police states or in near chaos. Our system is not perfect, but it has allowed for amazing creativity, scientific excellence, and personal growth and achievement. This shining light of freedom must be preserved and protected, lest we fall back into a dark age. Don't believe me? Ask anyone in China to discuss politics. Step outside that fancy hotel in Beijing and ask why no one dares to criticize the government.

Many of the threats to our great nation, our standard of living, and our traditions come not from the outside, but from internal issues. Consumerism runs amuck; that which focuses only on initial retail price without considering quality or the conditions in which the goods were produced, has long-term consequences. We send money abroad to buy not investments in our future, but cheap consumer goods. We then borrow hundreds of billions of our own dollars back every year to sustain our consumption. If we were borrowing to build something for the future—roads, universities, schools, hospitals, factories, power plants, and so on—it could be excusable, even reasonable. Unfortunately, the borrowing is nearly all for consumption of the moment, poured into low-quality goods that will be used up or discarded long before the interest on that debt is paid.

In *The Art of War*, Sun Tzu—a Chinese general (circa 544–496 BC)—wrote, "If you know the enemy and know yourself, you need not fear the result of a hundred battles."[1] For him, politics and war were both tools of national policy. Today, we must include economics as such a tool. Without question, trade is being used to push national goals and grow future superpowers. Our naive view that free trade among nations is good under any circumstances puts us at a huge disadvantage.

And the damage isn't purely economic. The apathy that this cheap consumerism encourages weakens our core values. Fewer people bother to stand for what is right, or even remember that we were once a nation governed by strong principles and ideals. We were a diverse nation with conflicting views, but people cared. In the end, we would come together as a people and fix real problems. Together, we fought Nazi Germany and Imperial Japan at the same time in World War II, threw off the yoke of the Great Depression, and became freedom's champion.

Our outlook today is bleak, but our problems are not as severe as those we faced during World War II. We still have time to act, and the ability to turn the tide. But that time is running out. Ignoring problems of this magnitude is like ignoring cancer. In many cases, it can be cured if it is identified and attacked early, but the longer one waits, the stronger the disease's foothold. Possible treatments become harsher and more risky until, eventually, there is no cure at all.

For me, there was no escaping these truths. Although I was personally getting richer, my country was, and still is, getting poorer. It was easy, even tempting, to turn a blind eye to it. But in the end, we are defined by the choices we make.

My choice meant leaving behind a lucrative executive role at an American technology company to start my own venture. That company would serve as a vehicle to challenge the deficit model and give people an actual choice, a business dedicated to nothing short of helping America to keep her manufacturing capability. Every day, we are able to make a real difference to our suppliers and our country. Thanks to those who visit the Web site (MadeinUSAForever.com) and our suppliers, there is meaning and purpose in every exhausting, yet exhilarating minute of it! Remember when that's what our great country was all about? Sadly, that feeling and the commitment that inspires it have slipped away from many of us; but it can be reclaimed.

No matter what your profession, your income level, your age, or your geography, you can take action and make a difference. This book will help you begin to see how, but it's just a beginning. As your focus shifts to the future, you'll discover new ways to put your beliefs into action every step of the way. The knowledge I have gained helps me every day; at the same time, I was quick to discover a new sort of modesty when I realized the vast amount I still needed to know to run a small business effectively and efficiently. Some lessons can be learned in books, but most have to be learned in practice. Nothing teaches like doing or creating.

The first step, the most important step, is simply to decide that you're ready to live consciously, to think about the future of the USA and of the children who will have to live with what we create, what we leave behind. Executives in other nations are nationalistic: They are Koreans first if they are Korean; Japanese first if they are from Japan. Toyota invests twice as much in Japan as in the United States—although the company sells more cars in this country than its own. Why is that? The Japanese never forget who they are or where their future lies, whereas American executives talk about ethics even as they shift millions of jobs to Asia.

Henry Ford, who had a lot of strengths and weaknesses, created an affordable car and paid his employees enough to buy it. He helped create his own customer base and bolstered the early American middle class. Today's executives, in contrast, are killing off their own customer base as they eliminate middle-class jobs, and then look to Washington for a bailout. We truly need to shake up the boardrooms around America. I have some ideas. . . .

The problems we face as a people are many, and we have all contributed to them. Business contributes, consumers contribute; and, sadly, even those in government, charged with protecting the USA and its people, are often part of the problem. A trade policy originally instituted to deal with friendly countries like Canada and the United Kingdom, or to bolster Japan and Korea against the Russians and Chinese, is now being taken advantage of on a massive scale by countries that are hardly our friends. It is no surprise they are from places like China, where massive pollution and lack of worker safety is the rule. Turning a blind eye to history means we are ignoring obvious lessons that should have allowed the United States to grow and lead the world in a new age of freedom—for centuries, not just a few decades. As much as I love the USA, ignoring history seems to be one of the things we do (or don't do?) best. Other nations know better. They watch in disbelief as we lurch forward, making mistakes such as spending more than $1 trillion on the war in Iraq, mystery stimulus plans, and other budget busters. All of this and more inspired me to write this book, and drove the creation of MadeinUSAForever.com.

The book is divided into three parts: "The Challenges We Face," "How America's Competitors Are Taking Advantage of Us," and "Rebuilding American Manufacturing."

Part I, "The Challenges We Face" encompasses a discussion of the current economic threat to our way of life; a brief historic discussion of how our politicians and business leaders have ceded our advantages; an overview of the historically unprecedented twin deficits in energy and production, and how they are gutting our economy; an explanation as to why service industry jobs can't, and won't, replace manufacturing as the backbone of the U.S. economy; and an introduction to the two wildly disparate possibilities for our future as a country.

In Part II, "How America's Competitors Are Taking Advantage of Us," I discuss our place in the world, from both a business and political standpoint, and share my firsthand observations of Beijing's awareness of the importance of manufacturing power to the political arena, and effectiveness in acting upon it. This part also addresses free and fair trade and describes how the playing field is stacked against us by foreign governments; here, I give actual examples of how many of our own retailers not only prefer to buy from sources that result in job loss for this country, but will seek out the absolute cheapest places to make products, despite egregious exploitation of those peoples and places.

Part III, "Rebuilding American Manufacturing" shifts the focus to what we are doing right and how we can turn our natural strengths as Americans into direct action, individually and as a collective. Finally, I discuss what the government can do, and what some great American companies are already doing, to restore our place in the world.

The situation, as I said, is dire; as you read this book, you will undoubtedly find some of the facts disheartening, and recent developments discouraging. But America's spirit and gumption are alive and well—the same spirit that carried us through World War II, the Great Depression, and many other threats to our way of life. From those challenges, we emerged victorious and went on to greater heights. We can, and will, do it again—but only if we make the decision, today, to invest in our own future.

In the end, it is not about what China or any other country does or does not do. It is about the route we choose. Do we take the difficult path today or the one that looks easy from where we stand today but that will be much rockier tomorrow? One road leads to a place where we fulfill our own destiny to renew our nation's greatness. The other carries us through inaction to ultimate collapse. Today, we stand at the crossroads; we have the opportunity to choose the path to greatness, to a secure and prosperous future.

Are you with me?

One

The Challenges
America Faces

Chapter 1 Why Buying American Is Critical

Why is the massive trade imbalance a critical problem for you and me?

With so many immediate problems facing us, personally and as a society, it's easy to ignore broad and seemingly distant problems. But many of the challenges we face as a nation today—a decaying economy, unemployment, falling wages, lack of opportunity, spiraling government debt, fractures spreading through every level of our economy—can be traced back to one source: the massive trade deficit. Our immediate personal issues, and the larger issues facing our country, are intimately related, and so are the solutions.

Recessions are getting longer and deeper. We are facing more, and more extended, periods of high unemployment. Even those who did everything right may spend months or even years unemployed (see Figure 1.1). So-called experts eager to calm our collective nerves talk about "jobless recoveries" and other such nonsense, but the concept is just that—nonsense.

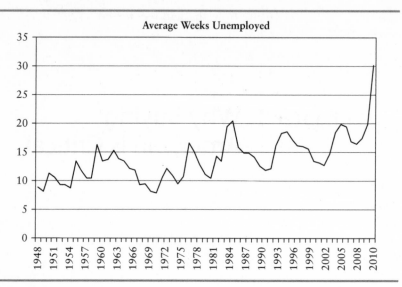

FIGURE 1.1 Labor Force Statistics from the Current Population Survey

The simple fact that we are not trading in a sustainable way with other countries impacts jobs, wages, product safety, and many other areas of our daily lives. The reality of our economic decline has already affected millions of people and will hit tens of millions more in the near future.

This is not just theory for huge numbers of our citizens. People all around us are being hit, and hit hard, through no fault of their own. One acquaintance, a CPA who had built a solid career, faced nearly two years of unemployment after losing his job early in the most recent downturn. The loss had nothing to do with his performance; the company simply had shrunk so significantly that there was no way to avoid being cut. In his midfifties and with kids in college, he was forced to spend much of his savings just when he should have been shoring up for retirement. He recently accepted a job where he makes about 40 percent less than he did in his previous job.

A customer who called MadeinUSAForever.com mentioned to me that she is the primary caretaker for her 15-year-old granddaughter, and that her work hours have been cut significantly. Fortunately, she has not lost her job—yet—but the reduced pay has caused a very real problem, and she is unsure how she will pay for her granddaughter's braces. But her worst fear is losing that job.

These are just two examples among many. Every one of us knows good, hardworking people facing similar hardships. Wages are down, and many of those who have managed to find jobs after extended unemployment are earning only 50 to 60 percent of what they used to make. Most of us could find ourselves in that position, abruptly out of a job despite solid performance, and with nothing but a year or two of unemployment standing between us and hard times.

Our deindustrialization exacerbates another growing problem. Many local and state governments—and, soon, even the federal government—are facing a severe lack of tax revenue cash coming in. If something doesn't change quickly, these government entities will soon find themselves unable to fulfill pension commitments, or provide even basic services. Our federal government has already had to borrow heavily from foreigners, and is becoming more dependent on them every year (see Figures 1.2, 1.3, and 1.4).

We hear "there's no easy answer," and that may be true, but there is a simple one. In most cases, the economic activity that manufacturing creates would generate the revenues necessary to support our cities and states. Without that activity, governments at every level

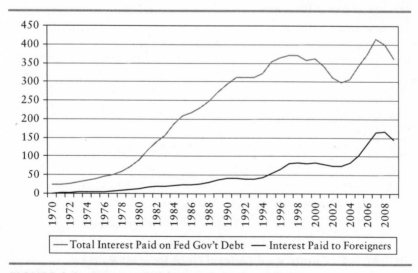

FIGURE 1.2   Interest Paid on U.S. Federal Debt
Data Source: Bureau of Economic Analysis.

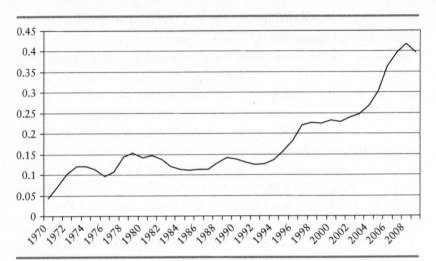

FIGURE 1.3   Percentage of Federal Debt Interest Paid to Foreigners
Data Source: Bureau of Economic Analysis.

will face permanently lower tax revenue collections, which will crimp their ability to borrow, causing many to collapse financially. Financial collapse would mean a depression era for decades to come, marked by extremely high unemployment rates, low wages where there are jobs, and even hunger for many.

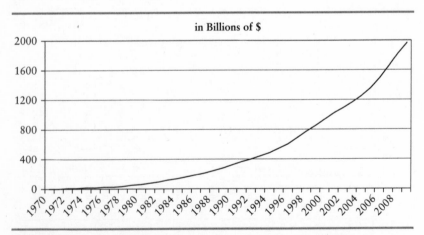

FIGURE 1.4   Cumulative Federal Debt Interest Paid to Noncitizens (1970–2009)
Data Source: Bureau of Economic Analysis.

It's tempting to blame the federal budget deficit on overspending in Washington, but the truth is more complex, with multiple factors coming into play. A lack of tax revenue coming in the door, due to a declining economy, limits the ability of any governmental entity to do its job. Raising taxes may seem like the solution to some, but with the decline in both employment and average wages, the income available for taxing has also declined. And in a faltering economy, increasing taxes does further harm, since consumers then have even less disposable income to feed into the system. Every year, hundreds of billions of dollars leave our country to pay for imports. With more strategic spending, those dollars could help to rebuild our economy, crumbling infrastructure, or educational system. No nation's economy can withstand that kind of wealth transfer for long, and we're seeing clear signs that we've reached the breaking point.

Our middle class is already fading. We once took it for granted that our children would lead better lives than we did, yet today many young people look at their parents' jobs with the envy of those who have witnessed something that can never be theirs.

Many once-great cities are facing unemployment rates so high that disenchantment grows. In some, unemployment rates for people under 30 are at 30 to 40 percent. A significant sector of the generation we need to lead our country into the future has no stake in our society, and little or no personal experience to demonstrate that working hard and creating quality products is in any way tied to personal or collective success. Those young people with no vested interest in our society have little to lose, and thus are more susceptible to involvement in crime and drugs. A few short decades of massive deficits have taken us from a golden age to an era of growing despair. That's why it's so critical that we act now to reduce the trade deficit by buying American-made products, and that we begin immediately, before the situation spirals further out of control.

This is not a detached concept or a philosophical political issue best left to those in academia to sort out. The choices you and I make every day, every time we step up to a checkout counter or place an order online, affect the future of the United States, our personal economic futures, and the kind of world our children will live in.

In later chapters, I'll talk in more depth about specific problems and possible solutions, but first let's look at the basics: the top 10 reasons

I believe you should buy products made here in the USA, as listed on MadeinUSAForever.com.

10. FOREIGN LABOR STANDARDS ALLOW UNSAFE WORKER CONDITIONS IN MANY COUNTRIES. WHEN YOU BUY AMERICAN, YOU SUPPORT NOT ONLY AMERICAN MANUFACTURERS BUT ALSO AMERICAN WORKERS, SAFE WORKING CONDITIONS, AND CHILD LABOR LAWS.

At Chinese factories, even "model" facilities used by contractors that build for Apple, HP, and others similar, suicide is common. I know from experience in the technology industry and working in Asia that these contract manufacturers bid below cost to win deals with well-known companies like Apple. After they win the contract, they put extreme pressure on their employees to drive down their costs to a point at which the contract is profitable. Again, that's at the "good" factories! I have seen Chinese contract manufacturers take it a step further: They make up for losing money by passing work to subcontractors that cut every corner. Working conditions are far worse at these subcontractors—which, in fact, make up the majority of the actual production. Those subcontractors may then push production even further down the line, to smaller subcontractors, until the original maker has little connection to the process and no ability to oversee quality or working conditions. With each step, those conditions deteriorate further.

Often, local government officials are not just on the payroll, but own shares in the local companies where dangerous conditions prevail. We might expect that those officials would be cautious, given their reputations are on the line; instead, the lack of government protection for workers remains at least as lax as it is in other factories. Sometimes, conditions are considerably worse, since the management feels safe from prosecution. By purchasing these products, we reward and perpetuate abusive working conditions.

More than 2,600 people "officially" died in Chinese coal mining accidents in 2009. Fires, floods, gas, electrical accidents—the causes ran the gambit—but the reason, across the board, was serious worker safety issues. The actual numbers are probably much higher, as many mines operate without an official license. Buying products created under these conditions is neither ethical nor consistent with concerns about worker safety and the value of human life.

9. JOBS SHIPPED ABROAD ALMOST NEVER RETURN. WHEN YOU BUY GOODS MADE IN THE USA, YOU HELP KEEP THE AMERICAN ECONOMY GROWING.

Previous recessions meant factories slowed down to one shift, or even briefly stood idle; but now these factories are disappearing by the thousands, and are not coming back. The difference between cutting back and closing is critical: Once a factory closes completely, it rarely reopens. The machinery is typically shipped overseas or scrapped, leaving local economies devastated. It is very hard for a community to regrow its local economy. When a large number of skilled positions are eliminated in an area, the skill base of the former employees starts to fade almost immediately, and valuable skill sets are lost forever.

For example, one of the major factors in our victory in World War II was our ability to build and transport a massive volume of materials and weapons. The "Liberty Ships," with the capacity to carry more than 10,000 tons at a range of 23,000 miles, made that possible. Eighteen shipyards around our nation built more than 2,700 of these ships in four years, a phenomenal display of industrial aptitude, power, and gumption, which our enemies could not hope to match.[1] Those shipyards are mostly closed today, and the skilled workers long gone.

Today's unemployed are spending not weeks or even months, but years between jobs. Skills rust, new technology renders them obsolete, and the once-skilled laborer must essentially start from scratch. Most of them were good employees who worked hard and did nothing wrong, but their specialized skills that once were valuable to the manufacturer often do not translate to qualification for available jobs. The ability to make advanced tooling carries no weight when the only job opening is "Wal-Mart greeter." Likewise, Wal-Mart and other companies of its ilk do not teach skills that prepare employees for the kind of work America needs.

When a factory closes, the emotional and financial toll it takes on displaced employees and their families is compounded by the heavy impact it has on the community. High levels of unemployment lead to an increase in foreclosure rates, lowering property values and creating dangerous pockets where many homes are vacant. The decreased purchasing power of local residents directly affects the sustainability of local businesses, whose closing in turn triggers even higher unemployment rates. As serious as this consequence has been in isolated communities in the past, the worst has yet to come. As economic conditions continue to worsen, and more manufacturers are either driven out of business or opt to ship operations overseas, the devastation we have seen in isolated communities will spread to impact states, regions, even the country as a whole.

8. U.S. MANUFACTURING PROCESSES ARE MUCH CLEANER FOR THE ENVIRONMENT THAN THOSE IN MANY OTHER COUNTRIES; MANY BRANDS SOLD HERE ARE PRODUCED IN COUNTRIES USING DANGEROUS, HEAVILY POLLUTING PROCESSES. WHEN YOU PURCHASE AMERICAN-MADE PRODUCTS, YOU KNOW THAT YOU'RE HELPING TO KEEP THE WORLD A LITTLE CLEANER FOR YOUR CHILDREN.

Moving production abroad nearly always means a significant increase in pollutants being released into the environment. Manufacturers in the USA are subject to environmental regulation, and meeting or exceeding those requirements is a primary cost of doing business. Due to much looser standards—not to mention the ease of bribing local government officials—manufacturers in countries like China are able to produce the same items more cheaply, while producing and releasing more pollution. I saw appalling amounts of pollution spewing into the air and water in China. Walking the capital, I was shocked to see after blowing my nose that the tissue was black with what looked like soot.

The maker saves the short-term cost of protecting the environment, while ignoring the price the polluting nation and the rest of the world will pay in the long term. Many Americans pay lip service to environmental concerns, but there is no point in pretending we care about the environment if we continue to buy products from heavy-polluting nations. If a person really cares about nature and the environment, he or she should buy from nations that enforce pollution controls at least as strict as those in this country.

Additionally, the pollution caused just from transporting those cheap goods across the ocean is huge. According to *The Guardian*,[2] just 15 of those enormous cargo container ships produce as much pollution as all the cars in the world. Transportation of goods within the United States is regulated heavily for pollution emissions, whereas the lack of standards in overseas transit means these vessels use the cheapest, dirtiest fuel available, spewing 2,000 times the level of sulfur and other pollutants. This is not just an environmental tragedy; it's also a ridiculous, unfair cost advantage over our domestic manufacturers.

7. MANY COUNTRIES HAVE NO MINIMUM WAGE RESTRICTIONS, OR THE MINIMUM WAGE IS OUTRAGEOUSLY LOW. WHEN YOU CHOOSE PRODUCTS MADE IN THE USA, YOU CONTRIBUTE TO THE PAYMENT OF AN HONEST DAY'S WAGES FOR AN HONEST DAY'S WORK.

Another key reason some goods made abroad are cheaper than those produced here is that the wages paid in some nations are barely above subsistence level—or even below. Even if there is a minimum wage, many companies ignore it or find ways to get around it. For example, lingerie factories have appeared along the border shared by Thailand and Myanmar (aka: Burma), to take advantage of the influx of political and economic refugees. The makers there hire mostly desperate women at very low wages, and even force them to pay a significant portion of their income as rent, to live in so-called company dormitories.

Subcontracting, a system of using less formal producers, taking work from bigger companies in these nations, results in even more serious wage abuse. Production is farmed out as piecemeal work, such as sewing a thousand shirts per week per household, and it leads to an effective pay rate well below minimum wage, and even child labor abuses in some places.

This sort of drastically low wage is vital for the chain stores that sell disposable goods at "low, low" prices. Sadly, women working in horrid conditions in the Thai jungle, producing hundreds of millions of bras and panties, are often turning out products sold so cheaply that many buyers here think nothing of dropping them in the garbage at the first sign of wear.

We are taught to believe that this constitutes "development" in those nations, but the lack of sustainable jobs created in the long run argues against that point. These facilities are not even permanent. As this source of cheap labor dries up, the equipment is moved to the next hot spot.

6. THE GROWING LACK OF U.S. CAPABILITY TO MANUFACTURE MANY PRODUCTS IS STRATEGICALLY UNSOUND. WHEN YOU SEEK OUT AMERICAN-MADE GOODS, YOU FOSTER AMERICAN INDEPENDENCE.

During World War II, the battle for Midway was the turning point of the war against Imperial Japan. We lost the aircraft carrier York-town, but the Japanese lost four major aircraft carriers—a blow they were never able to recover from. That's old news to many history buffs, but do you know how many new aircraft carriers each country added after Midway? Japan was able to add only six for the rest of the war. The USA? *Seventeen* major fleet aircraft carriers were produced and sent to the Pacific alone, with others going to Europe.[3] We outproduced the Japanese more than three to one. That enabled us to the take the war to their homeland in just a few years. Could we do that today? Do we have the skills, shipyards, tooling, steel, and the rest? We would be very hard-pressed to meet the supply needs of an extended war against a "real" power. We have our hands full with little Afghanistan.

To make matters worse, modern weapon systems require components that we are not even making. Microprocessors, advanced materials, and electronic components must be imported.

It is strategically unsound for a great power to be unable to produce what it needs to defend itself. History shows that this inability is a sure sign of decline. The Spanish and Roman empires both hollowed out after losing their ability to produce necessities domestically. What took centuries to die out in those declining empires, however, we have managed to give away in just a couple of decades.

One thing is certain in history: It always repeats. The names and faces are different, but the cycles of peace and war, feast and famine, justice and darkness always rerun. To believe that we will not face another power someday, one that is 10 times stronger than Iraq and Afghanistan combined, is to be as ignorant of human history as one is optimistic.

It is critical that we are ready to face such a challenge. In fact, being ready is the ultimate deterrent. No bully wants to get his butt kicked. He smells weakness and goes after those less able to defend themselves. Not long ago, it would have been beyond our imagination that the United States would be a country that smelled of weakness. But being ready means having an industrial base in place so that we can make what we need to defend ourselves, and then to take the fight to the enemy and win. That base is not firmly in place today, and the situation is steadily worsening. Reliance on other countries, particularly those that do not share our beliefs, is precisely the kind of weakness that attracts the bully.

5. THE HUGE U.S. TRADE DEFICIT LEADS TO MASSIVE, UNSUSTAINABLE BORROWING FROM OTHER COUNTRIES. DEBT ISN'T GOOD FOR YOU AND IT ISN'T GOOD FOR AMERICA.

Our trade deficit has drained more than $9 trillion dollars from the USA between 1974 and 2009.[4] Within the same time frame, our federal budget deficit has increased from $4 trillion to $12 trillion. That's no coincidence. Other nations protect their trade surpluses because they understand the positive economic effect of manufacturing. That puts them in the position of strength, able to loan our money back to us. We have turned into the world's debtor nation (see Figure 1.5).

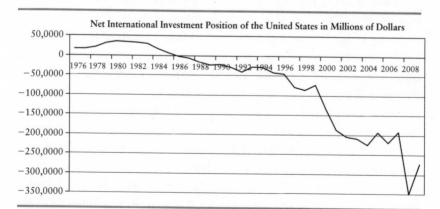

FIGURE 1.5   The USA Becomes a Debtor Nation
Data Source: Bureau of Economic Analysis.

A dollar of manufacturing activity is, in fact, worth more than a dollar. Not only the company's employees, but also their suppliers, the suppliers' employees, and many others in the chain of production and transportation benefit. That creates a multiplier effect: $1.00 in manufacturing activity here is actually worth $1.70, when the activity of suppliers and all other support is added in. As if the $10 trillion trade deficit weren't serious enough, the deficit actually means that the USA lost out on $17 trillion in economic activity. At least 40 percent of that $17 trillion would have been collected at some point as tax revenue in the country where items are manufactured. That means nearly $7 trillion of tax revenue has been lost in that 35-year period because we did not produce items here. Of the $8 trillion federal budget deficit in those 35 years, $7 trillion, or 87 percent, could have been naturally covered by increased economic activity if we had just had balanced trade.

What would that $7 trillion have meant to the USA? As we pay about 4 percent interest on that debt, that $7 trillion means about $280 billion in extra interest we have to pay on the federal budget deficit every year! That is an extra $1,000-plus in interest payments alone for every man, women, and child in this country—and that doesn't even take into account the impact of compound interest. This paralyzing debt has become a severe burden on our economy and way of life. Imagine how much richer we would be today as a people and a nation if the trade deficit had never been allowed to grow like that!

China, Korea, Japan, and to a lesser degree, Germany, treat the United States like a surplus export dumping ground. No other nation or group of nations would have been able to absorb so many imports for so long. But even a country as large and once-wealthy as ours has limits. Japan and China talk about exporting to each other, but what they're talking about is components, many of which are being reexported to the USA. They look out for their own interests first, driving their economies through exports to the USA, then turning around and loaning our money back to us. Mathematically, these trade and budget deficits cannot continue much longer.

It was not invasion of the homeland that signaled the Spanish Empire's collapse in the seventeenth century. It was financial ruin caused by its inability pay its debts. Today, the United States is teetering dangerously near to that same position.

4. FOREIGN PRODUCT SAFETY STANDARDS ARE LOW. FOR EXAMPLE, POISONOUS LEVELS OF LEAD ARE IN TENS OF MILLIONS OF TOYS SHIPPED TO THIS COUNTRY. WHEN YOU BUY TOYS AND OTHER GOODS MADE IN THE USA, YOU CAN BE CONFIDENT THAT AMERICAN CONSUMER PROTECTION LAWS AND SAFETY STANDARDS ARE IN PLACE TO PROTECT YOUR FAMILY.

In 2007, toy manufacturer Mattel recalled tens of millions of toys due to the presence of dangerous levels of lead. All of those toys were made outside the USA, the vast majority in China. So great is the dependence of some American companies on cheap overseas labor, however, that although the Chinese manufacturers were responsible for the toxins, still today tens of millions of toys are imported from China. Since the 2007 toy recall, there have been more problems with dangerous chemicals, in imported food (both for humans and animals), drywall, and again in toys.

If an unsafe item is made in the USA, the maker may face lawsuits or even go to jail. Recourse is less clear when imported products prove dangerous. In the case of Chinese-produced drywall, for example, folks who either bought homes or had remodeling done between 2006 and 2008 are coping with dangerous levels of hydrogen sulfide so high that the Centers for Disease Control and Prevention is recommending the drywall be torn out.[5] The damage and health costs are significant, and U.S. drywall makers would have been liable had they created the dangerous materials. But the manufacturers of these poisonous materials are out of reach. Nearly all those whose homes were contaminated by Chinese drywall are unable to get those Chinese companies into court, much less successfully prosecute claims against them.

No one is checking the cargo containers that come in through our ports for dangerous products or chemicals, and hundreds of thousands come through each day. It's difficult to understand what could be more important to our own government than the health and safety of its citizens, yet we see little or no action on the issue. Not only is this a real threat to our children's health, but ironically, it also puts domestic manufacturers at an extreme cost disadvantage. Since foreign producers are not held to the same standards, their cost of production is substantially lower.

Imports must be safe to be allowed into our nation. They must at the very least meet our own standards. This grievous situation must be addressed. Yet our own behaviors and those of our corporations and even our government perpetuate the benefits of producing goods cheaply and without safety standards. Only when we stop purchasing dangerous goods from overseas will we be able to have confidence in the quality of the goods we bring into our homes. We may hope that our government will intervene and encourage that change; we may hope that corporate America will step up and stop purchasing these faulty goods, and we may call on them to do so. In the end, though, there's just one piece of the process that's wholly within our control, right now: We don't have to buy those questionable goods.

3. LACK OF MINIMUM WAGE, WORKER SAFETY, OR ENVIRONMENTAL POLLUTION CONTROLS IN MANY COUNTRIES UNDERMINES THE CONCEPT OF "FAIR AND FREE TRADE." NO WESTERN NATION CAN ULTIMATELY COMPETE ON PRICE WITH A COUNTRY WILLING TO EXPLOIT ITS OWN PEOPLE AND POLLUTE ITS OWN ENVIRONMENT ON A MASSIVE SCOPE. WHEN YOU BUY ONLY AMERICAN-MADE PRODUCTS, YOU INSIST ON A HIGHER STANDARD.

Our government sets a minimum wage for our workers, and apparently expects other governments to do their share for their own people. But what if those foreign countries don't?

I've already discussed the fact that many nations are perfectly willing to exploit their people and use the police to keep a lid on trouble; we have seen the impact that exploitation has on the quality of life for those workers and in those countries. The minimum wage is $0.29 per hour in Vietnam.[6] And that's a best-case scenario; in practice, even those low minimums often are not enforced. Additionally, a much larger portion of the workforce is working for minimum wage in those nations. The disparity between our nations is dramatic. A U.S.-based company paying a minimum of $7.25/hour has a hard time competing with a company based in Vietnam paying just over 4 percent. The U.S.-based company providing a sustainable living for its employees will always have a higher cost of production than those of foreign companies, and that's without factoring in the additional costs associated with environmental regulation and worker safety. We need to consider a worldwide minimum wage, one that is likely well below our USA standard today, but ensures some level of basic living standard in other countries.

The standards that determine which countries we'll buy from are difficult to understand. The concept of "free and fair trade" does not address these unfair cost advantages, particularly when power exporter nations are determined to take business and jobs and absorb factories on almost any terms.

2. FACTORIES AND MONEY ARE SHIFTING TO COUNTRIES NOT FRIENDLY TO THE USA OR DEMOCRACY. WHEN YOU AVOID IMPORTED GOODS IN FAVOR OF AMERICAN-MADE ITEMS, YOU HELP ENSURE THAT THE UNITED STATES DOESN'T FIND ITS ACCESS TO VITAL GOODS HINDERED BY POLITICAL CONFLICT.

China, Vietnam, and particularly the oil exporters Saudi Arabia, Iran, and Venezuela stand against democracy and world freedom. By allowing our factories to move to these nations, and by indulging our addiction to foreign oil, we are abandoning our ability to produce; instead, we are handing it over to nations that could turn against us in the future. The continued reduction (or even disappearance) of manufacturing power in the United States could leave us entirely dependent on nations we know we cannot rely on. How will we continue to be the "arsenal of freedom," as we were in World War I and World War II?

Slowly but surely, foreign governments are moving into a position to dictate terms to us, particularly in Washington, due to our national debt. Imagine the position the USA will be in when the next world crisis arises. If China were to attack Taiwan five years from now, would our leaders be in any position to stand up and object?

We have a lot of antiquated military equipment left over from the Cold War that has helped us deal with recent small wars. The last B-52 was produced by Boeing in 1962,[7] but it is still the backbone of our bomber fleet. Surely, there is a limit to the number of years and the number of wars through which this outdated equipment can sustain us. When we reach that limit, we may be in for a rude awakening.

Whether we need electronics—which are already being manufactured abroad almost exclusively—or some sort of synthetic materials to absorb radar waves, or really good, inexpensive body armor, or some state-of-the-art technology we haven't yet imagined, we will not be able to produce it without factories.

1. AS U.S. MANUFACTURING CAPABILITY FADES, FUTURE GENERATIONS OF U.S. CITIZENS WILL BE UNABLE TO FIND RELEVANT JOBS. BUY AMERICAN AND HELP KEEP YOUR FRIENDS, FAMILY, AND NEIGHBORS, AND EVEN YOURSELF, EARNING A LIVING WAGE.

One of the widest cracks in the foundation of our way of life is the employment crisis Americans face. Already, it is obvious that under the present circumstances we are unable to fully employ our people, much less help them to find relevant work. Make-work government jobs and stimulus welfare checks help an individual feed his or her family on a given day, but do nothing for his or her long-term prospects. More and more frequently I hear about people who have been unemployed for six months, a year, even going on two years. Multiyear unemployment is becoming frighteningly common. As savings, skills, and prospects fade, these folks eventually limp into jobs that pay a fraction of what they were making. These are not strangers anymore, and we can no longer pretend that it couldn't happen to us. We all know good people experiencing this fate. Some of us are undoubtedly among them.

An acquaintance with 40 years of work experience recently took a job at Wal-Mart, where he is making slightly more than minimum wage, because he could not find anything else. When a customer dented his car with a shopping cart, Wal-Mart told him that it was his problem. Another man I know, college educated, is delivering pizzas; a third is a real estate agent with no customers and a negative income. These aren't people who are unwilling to work, or who want to pick and choose; they're people just like you who are doing what they have to do to support themselves and their families, yet continuing to fall further behind.

What will tomorrow bring if even more factories close? The generation now moving through school and recent graduates face the worst job prospects since the Great Depression—not just for a year or two, but potentially for decades. It is unclear where the good jobs of the future will come from. Once upon a time, government jobs were the reliable fallback, but many city governments are already facing insolvency. State governments, and even our federal government, will soon face an increasingly dire financial situation. Governments can only raise money through taxes, printing, or borrowing, and all of these alternatives are becoming more and more limited. With pension benefits and basic services already at risk at some levels, few governmental entities will be in a position to create new jobs.

Our future is hazy. It's difficult to imagine what the next generation of Americans will do for a living, how they will find relevant work, let alone how they will establish the emotional stake in our way of life that makes true citizens. We are all letting them down: politicians, business leaders, and fellow citizens who choose low prices and convenience over American-made products. It's time we changed that. Each of these issues is a crack in the dam, and what was once "the American way of life" is already leaking away.

The good news is we still have time to act and really make a difference, if we commit ourselves to doing so. Yes, the cost in time and effort to remake the USA is high, but the financial and human cost of continued decay is much higher. This is not a TV episode or movie with a quick solution. There is no happy ending, unless we stand up and make real change happen—not over days, but years. Hope motivates, but doing is the key to achieving.

The choices we make today are critical to our future; critical to that worker who has been unemployed for two years; critical to the mother trying to feed her young kids; critical to the nurse visiting an aged retiree and wondering whether she will be paid; critical to that retiree wondering whether her pension is really safe. . . . Most of all it is critical to our nation's health as a whole. These issues will fester and become disastrous if sustainable solutions are not found and implemented.

We can continue to take the easy way for the moment. We can purchase the least expensive goods at the most convenient location without thinking about where those goods came from, what kind of toxins they might contain, at what cost to the environment they were manufactured, whether the person who assembled them was driven to suicide by the pressures of a pennies-per-day job, or what impact our decisions will have on the future of U.S. independence. Or we can once again become a nation where the sky is the limit; where ability and hard work matter; where jobs are restored, manufacturing retooled, and we are again able to compete with the world. We can live in a country where our children achieve far more than we ever dreamed; where foreign nations try not to attack us, but to emulate our freedoms and way of life; and where we lead as individuals and as a nation to a future of greatness, not decline.

It's in your hands. Which is it going to be?

Chapter 2 How This Happened

The Rise of the Power Exporters and Wal-Mart

In a few short decades, the USA has fallen from world industrial leader to industrial weakling, burdened by record trade and budget deficits. Looking honestly at that dramatic change may be painful, but it's necessary. If we're going to fix the problems facing our nation today, we need cold, hard facts. We also need to take a cold hard look at our real strengths and weaknesses as a nation, to understand what we've done right and what we've done wrong. Only then will we have the tools to turn the situation around.

Our economic leadership did not come crashing to an end overnight. It took several decades to give away such an incredible advantage, and the changes slipped right by many of us. Even now, some of you may be shocked that I am suggesting that our country is no longer the world leader. Sadly, that's one of those cold, hard facts we must come to terms with if we are to move forward.

There are five main reasons for our economic decline:

1. We let the power exporter nations—China, Korea, Japan, and Germany—take serious advantage of us.
2. Our retail chains, led by Wal-Mart, more than encouraged low-cost imports from abroad; in the process, they put their own American customers out of work.
3. Many of our business leaders from the post–World War II generation have dropped the ball.
4. Many of our own people have stopped caring where things are made, and do not even understand or care about the relationship between making items and jobs.
5. Finally, Washington has drifted farther and farther from responsible rule, and now must bear substantial blame for their ineptitude.

Up to World War I, the great powers at the time, including a young United States, knew the value of an effective manufacturing base. It was understood that manufacturing, jobs, and national power are intertwined. Post–World War II through about 1955, we had the world by the horns. Factories abroad had, in many cases, been destroyed or left unusable by the war, and our economy was surging. We even helped those nations rebuild, via the Marshall Plan and other assistance that gave our allies in Europe and Asia the resources to buy our grain and steel, and even the capability to rebuild their factories using the newest, most efficient manufacturing technology available. We knew then that industry was critical to rebuilding. In the past few decades, however, we, the United States, have taken our eyes off the ball. Other nations did not.

Our perception of our advantages turned into an arrogance that has endured in Washington much longer than it should have. When this country's original trading partners were primarily known entities like Canada, Latin America, and England, there was little threat to our modern industrial might. The rise of other real competitors, playing the game by their own rules, was largely ignored by our leaders.

> ## HEROES OF OUR USA EFFORT IN THEIR OWN WORDS
>
> ### Roger Simmermaker, Author and Union Machinist
>
> Making products in the USA is not only important to keep jobs in our country, but also to ensure profits stay here and tax revenue is paid to the U.S. Treasury instead of foreign treasuries. Foreign workers don't pay taxes to America; only American workers do. We must be able to pay for the things "We the People" have demanded from the use of our tax dollars.
>
> As the author of *How Americans Can Buy American: The Power of Consumer Patriotism,* Third Edition (Consumer Patriotism Corporation, 2008), printing and publishing my book anywhere but in America would be contrary to my deeply held beliefs—and hypocritical as well.
>
> Despite being undercut on price by foreign producers from lower-cost nations, I believe American workers are the best in the world, and most Americans feel the same. Studies have shown that when given a choice between an American product and a foreign one, when price and quality are the same, most Americans prefer American-made goods. And an April 21, 2010, Associated Press poll showed that more Americans now rate U.S.-made cars as having higher quality than Asian-built ones.
>
> Apart from the advantages of higher American employment, and therefore more affluent American consumers to buy American products, there are advantages in being closer to American customers. Quality control of production is easier when that production is local, when compared to the option of being a distant owner of a foreign factory.
>
> We must buy American now so there will always be American left to buy in the future. We cannot stop foreign companies from buying American companies, land, factories, and other assets (often, with money that used to be ours), but we can stop giving foreign companies and producers the money with which to do it.

For example, when I lived in Japan and Singapore, I talked to many Asian businesspeople who agreed that Washington purposely winked at trade surpluses with Japan and Korea throughout the 1960s because we were trying to bolster them to stand with us against the Soviets. They took full advantage. Korea, a country slightly larger than Indiana,[1] has more than $257 billion of our dollars in reserve[2] from the deficit we run with them. Japan, a country slightly smaller than California,[3] but with fewer natural resources, has $989 billion of our dollars in reserve.[4] Japan was the biggest foreign provider of

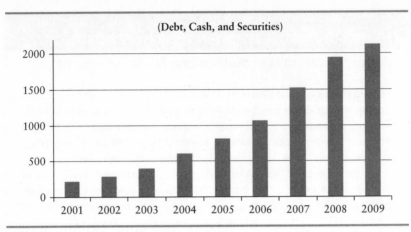

(Debt, Cash, and Securities)

FIGURE 2.1 China's Holdings of Billions of U.S. Dollar Reserves
Source: Congressional Research Service Report, "China's Holding of U.S. Securities: Implications for U.S. Economy," June 30, 2009.

loans to our government, until recently, when the Chinese claimed that title. China currently owns more than $2,132 billion of our dollars in reserve, including government debt and every type of asset (see Figure 2.1).[5] Yes, that is more than $2,000 billion!

Somehow, the advantages we gave the Japanese and Koreans became built in over the years, and even part of the "free trade" lingo. I have never encountered a businessperson in Asia who really

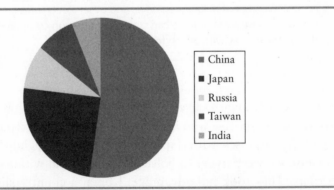

FIGURE 2.2 Top Foreign Reserve Holders in Billions of U.S. Dollars (as of June 2009)
Source: Congressional Research Service Report, "China's Holding of U.S. Securities: Implications for U.S. Economy," June 30, 2009.

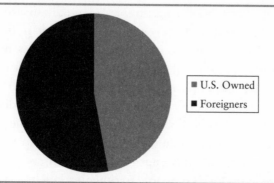

FIGURE 2.3   Percentage of U.S. Federal Debt Held by Foreigners (excluding that held by Social Security)
Source: Congressional Research Service Report, "China's Holding of U.S. Securities: Implications for U.S. Economy," June 30, 2009.

agrees with true "free trade." Many consider it a joke on us. Any American with experience in Asia will tell you how difficult it is to export to those nations. Why did Washington do little more than pay lip service to leveling the playing field again? The answer is simple, though disturbing: Foreign countries lobbying in Washington, our retailers' lobbying, and our leaders' weakness.

Over time, these deficits with Korea and Japan that we tolerated in order to help them to rebuild should have diminished. Instead, they became the norm. Talk to those in the know in both countries and they will readily admit that their nations are much less open to our products, and moreover, that our openness is unbelievable. They expect us to wise up in the near future and become a lot less open, an expectation that unfortunately hasn't seemed to match our behavior thus far. Most people here, even business and political leaders, are oblivious to, or deny, the history. They do not perceive the negative effect on our nation, or realize that we really can do something about it. It is not unusual, when discussing the USA's deficit situation in Asia, to see amusement or pride, or both in the eyes of our beneficiaries.

Much worse, China seized on the advantageous trade situation we instituted with our allies Japan and Korea. We allowed Korea and Japan these advantages in part to stop the spread of communism, yet the last and by far largest pseudo-communist nation in the world is now being permitted to gain the same benefits on the same terms.

China has used this boon to an unprecedentedly massive degree to fund and build its industry at every level. Still, we do nothing.

Germany, too, has driven its economy for decades by running a constant surplus of material good exports. Although it is not a low-wage nation, it makes up for it by implementing industrial processes that use fewer worker hours while maintaining high quality. The Germans know full well that this model cannot maintain the employment level they consider acceptable without an export surplus of goods or much higher domestic consumption. Their own consumption level per citizen remains low, compared to other leading industrial nations, meaning they cannot make up for a lower surplus by shipping more within their own country until their citizens learn to spend more.

The recoveries in Japan, Korea, and Germany were initially advantageous for the United States, as they were financial burdens just after the war, as well as being opportune allies in stopping the spread of communism. None of the three nations ever lost their commitment to having a strong economy based on manufacturing. Those surpluses paid many bills, and were the engines of their development. A surplus meant that for all those decades, from about 1950 through today, they were taking cash from other nations. The positive effect of the surpluses on those countries' economies was engendered largely by the high rate of the economic effect of manufacturing. Japan, Korea, and Germany know this, and they also know they are taking this money and the positive economic activity out from those nations that consistently run a deficit—rather like the characters in those silly vampire television shows suck blood out of innocent, if naïve, people. They are aware not just that they are taking too much out of the rest of the world, but also that their economies in their present forms are very much dependent on it. They have driven their economies to run the maximum surplus they can possibly get away with.

That is not to say that our constant deficits with these nations are their fault entirely. Washington allowed it, initially for political reasons, and then lost the understanding and the will to act. Too long in the sun, having staved off the threat of communism, our own leaders did not understand or care about the cancer spreading throughout our economy. But the system contains a fatal flaw. This codependence between the surplus nations and the deficit nations can last only as long as the deficit nations have, or can borrow, money.

We seem to have forgotten that we winked at Japan's and Korea's surpluses because they were "on the front" and would take the brunt of the fighting if communism continued to spread. Over a million people died in the Korean War alone. We lost 36,940 soldiers.[6] The vast majority of those killed in the Korean War were Korean civilians. It made sense to strengthen our allies in the south of Korea through direct aid and by allowing a trade surplus. Our military leaders and politicians encouraged it because doing so allowed the South Koreans to modernize without our directly paying for that modernization. But whether our leaders recognize it or not, indirect costs are still real costs.

South Korea has been playing the North Korea card ever since, although the need for us to permit it to take such a huge surplus from the United States has long since been reduced. Why is our duty to, in effect, pay for its defense today, even as we weaken our ability to provide for our own? The Korean War has been over for more than half a century. Yes, the North Koreans continue to be belligerent, and even downright odd, but is North Korea, the so-called Hermit Nation, still such a threat to us and the world today that we should close down American factories so that South Korea can continue to export freely to us? After five decades, I am beginning to sense that we are getting scammed.

At the end of World War II, Japan was completely bombed, drained, and exhausted from its efforts to conquer most of Asia. The feudalist spirit of the day, combined with modern machines, had enabled them to effectively push aside all resistance, until they made the mistake of attacking the United States at Pearl Harbor. American heroism, coupled with our massive industrial base, turned the tide. Our occupation force found Japan completely depleted, with many civilians even facing hunger. At this moment in history, though so many American families had lost at least one son in defeating the Japanese Empire, we decided to help, because the Soviets were growing more hostile, and it was the "right thing to do" for the people there. Japan had lost its northernmost territory to Stalin's troops at the end of the war. Communist agents were active in Japan, trying to undermine our weak puppet government. The United States, under General MacArthur's personal leadership, decided to reawaken Japan's industry to help us stand against the Soviets. Giant companies like

Mitsubishi, which had built the Zero, the troublesome fighter plane, were allowed to continue to exist; moreover, they were reinvigorated. This enabled us to reduce direct aid payments while empowering Japan to turn itself into a bastion of freedom and democracy in Asia, literally within sight of the Soviet Empire. Those goals for Japan were accomplished by roughly 1955. Somehow, the informal policy allowing them to sustain a surplus with us never got corrected, though we are now more than 60 years past the point of the original need. The impact of the South Korean surplus, although significant, pales in comparison to the price we pay for our continuing deficit relationship with Japan.

Germany, too, was depleted at the end of World War II, through both the war effort and the Allied bombing. Since Eastern Europe had been occupied by the Soviets in the last few years of the war, Germany was shrunk—actually, split—and had become the European frontier between East and West. To this day, the German state of East Prussia in the Baltic Sea is a part of Russia. Poor Poland, always the whipping boy in modern Europe, had its borders moved, with the Soviets absorbing its eastern territory, and its western border moving into German territory. Politically, it was expedient to rebuild Western Germany as quickly as possible, as a buffer against further Soviet expansion. Not only was Germany allowed to ramp up its export machine, but the United States provided hundreds of billions of dollars in aid to Germany and Western Europe via the Marshall Plan. Thus, we not only opened the door so they could move into world markets, we even provided the investment seed money so they could rebuild on a massive scale.

Nearly every other war in history in which there has been a clear winner and loser, the losers paid reparations in terms of cash, gold, slaves, material items, and very often territory. At the end of World War II, the Soviets demanded, and got, territory and material goods; yet we asked for nothing and, to boot, spent an untold fortune rebuilding our former enemies. We are still, to this day, defending them militarily. Such was the overwhelming advantage of our massive manufacturing economy that this must have seemed like small change. Who could challenge us in manufacturing in 1949?

Unfortunately, Washington never bothered to change direction as our advantages vanished. We even provided such massive assistance to England and France that they dropped all requests for war repara-tions. The World War I reparations Germany was forced to accept, mainly by England and France, were much too heavy, and did in part lead to the rise of the Nazis and World War II. There was political expedience in assuring our new friends were able to stand with us against the Soviets, as well as genuine benevolence of the USA to do things differently for mankind. However, there is a point at which benevolence becomes unnecessary and, ultimately, self-destructive. Circumstances have changed dramatically since 1949. Today, we need to look after our nation first and foremost. We need our own Marshall Plan. We need to put America first.

Our large retail chains are a very big part of the trade deficit issue. Wal-Mart is the largest single importer from China. It encourages the Asian surplus nations to export too much to the USA. The major retailers take it even further, seeking out the lowest conceivable pro-duction price location in the world, no matter what is going on there. In the procurement offices of the major chains, "Made in USA" is not only *not* a priority, it's a joke. Price is the only factor that matters to them, even at the cost of quality, poor working conditions, or, most importantly to me, the elimination of American jobs.

Several MadeinUSAForever.com suppliers at one point sold to Wal-Mart. Most tell a similar, and sad, story. Considering Wal-Mart's volume of sales, the makers approached the chain again and again. Eventually, the "lucky" ones got a working relationship with a buyer, an employee in Wal-Mart's procurement office, and eventually launched some sales to Wal-Mart. The buyer demanded an uncom-fortably low price, but the makers decided to go for it because Wal-Mart sells so many units. Despite the initially low price, Wal-Mart typically comes back several times a year asking the makers to "sharpen their pencils," meaning cut the price again. Many makers initially tried to comply with Wal-Mart's demands, but soon realized they could barely cover the cost of making the items, much less pay the fixed costs involved with running a factory, such as taxes, utilities, and maintenance.

Eventually, most makers start to push back on Wal-Mart's price reduction demands. Suddenly, the buyer surprises the maker with the news that there is a supplier in China, ready, willing, and able to beat the maker's prices. The maker wonders how its items could have been duplicated so completely and quickly, but dares not accuse Wal-Mart of having sent samples to China. At this point, some makers remind the buyer that their products are "Made in USA," at which point nearly all hear something like, "That dog don't hunt no more." Price is the only consideration; no thought is given to the American workers who will suffer when the makers move their businesses abroad, or the long-term impact on our economy.

At this point, the maker may or may not give up. Some hold out for a few more price cuts, but all eventually come to the point where their "pencils can no longer be sharpened" and walk away from this business. But they don't walk away unscathed. Unfortunately, the makers' other retail customers often notice the item at Wal-Mart and complain about the price, forcing the makers to lower the price to other main customers, hurting overall profit. And, of course, Wal-Mart is now offering the cheaper imported version of the items. Because the makers sold to Wal-Mart, however briefly, the market price for their products is now permanently lower.

Wal-Mart has been the most efficient among the big retailers at forcing the absolute lowest cost of goods, no matter where they are from around the world, but it is by no means alone. Consider the number of American-made products on the shelves at Target, JCPenney, Costco, and similar stores. All of these retailers have shown a massive growth rate in the amount they import. They have raced after each other like rats down a hole to try to get a cost advantage over one another.

The justification for this used to be that it helped to develop that other nation's economy; in fact, when the wages become slightly too high in one location, production will very rapidly be moved to another country. Textiles, the production of clothing and other items made of cloth, is a case in point. It used to be thought of as real development for a third-world nation when textile factories were set up locally. Theoretically, these factories could help these countries enter the modern age. However, under pressure from our own retailers, makers in Asia have become quite adept at moving these facilities to still other, cheaper, locations. Governments actually encouraged and even pursued these companies to set up operations. A few years ago, European Union (EU) quotas protected some small nations' nascent industries, but when China was allowed to join the World Trade

Organization (WTO), in 2001, it vaporized much of the textile industry in places like Madagascar. The one exception was the items
requiring a high degree of cheap labor; in those situations, ultralow-
labor-cost nations like Vietnam have taken a big share of the market.

Furthermore, each of these industries impacts other sectors of our
economy in ways that most people never consider. For example, the
textile industry isn't just about cutting and sewing cloth. Textile mills
were once huge employers in the northeastern and southern United
States, and those mills in turn required components, equipment, and
services provided by other suppliers. (If we don't have textile mills,
who will buy the cotton farmers' crops?) Next, the designers and the
brands themselves potentially employ tens of thousands, even before
the sewing starts. Then comes the cutting and sewing, once performed
not in some sweatshop in the middle of a jungle, but by hardworking
Americans glad to have that paycheck. Then come the distribution
and logistics jobs: additional tens of thousands of folks working
toward creating and transporting that clothing, all before the retailers
even touch it! Everyone needs clothes. Done right, the textile industry
is a positive and important economic force in any nation.

The retailers are the next link in the chain between the maker
and the consumer. They have something of a special place in that relationship because the consumer actually sees the item on their shelves,
and they use that perceived power to put foreign products in front of
that individual. In search of a slightly lower cost, they were, and are,
willing to destroy the entire American supply chain that had been
loyal to them—in some cases, for generations. However, the real
power in the retailer-consumer relationship does not lie with the
retailer. It lies with the customer, because the customer makes
the choice whether to buy or not. If customers are aware that a
retailer has behaved in ways that violate their ethical beliefs, many
will take their business elsewhere. Each person can make the active
choice to buy at another store, or through a catalog or the Internet.

I founded MadeinUSAForever.com specifically to give folks the
option of researching and buying American-made products if they so
choose. It's easy to believe that your purchasing decisions don't make
a difference, that your money doesn't make up enough of a retailer's
income to be noticed. If every person who cared about these issues but
has felt that his or her spending decisions were too small to count

suddenly decided to act on those beliefs—if even a small percentage did—the net impact would definitely gain attention. You may have noticed that your grocery store has been stocking a lot of organic food lately, even if you shop at a large chain store. That's not because the store is concerned about your health; and it's certainly not because it's easier and cheaper to get organic produce. No, the stores have made space and found suppliers for those organic options because people cared enough to make it incumbent upon stores to offer organic food. Customers bothered them about it, making requests and issuing complaints in person, or sending e-mails, to let the stores know what they wanted. Some also voted with their dollars, seeking out farmers' markets or other options for obtaining healthier organic foods. In the end, grocers realized that if they wanted to retain that market sector, they would have to offer the healthier choices customers demanded.

We could accomplish the same thing with regard to American-made products. If enough of us made enough noise, the major retailers would start carrying a lot more products made here in the USA, just as they have begun to do with organic products. The retailers that focused even a tiny portion of their buying power on ensuring their products were American-made would make a big difference to those makers and their suppliers. Moreover, it would increase awareness and, thus, the opportunity for more Americans to choose goods made in the USA.

Over time, many U.S. consumers have become desensitized to buying American-made. They don't think about where items are made or consider the direct relationship between buying American-made and jobs or wages. Other countries, like Canada and Australia, teach this basic economic theory in school, and ingrain in the students' consciousness why it is better to buy items made in their home nation whenever possible.

This mind-set was second nature to everyone from the World War II generation in this country, but started to slip in the late sixties and seventies. Japanese cars made a real breakthrough in the early seventies because they were more fuel-efficient, for the simple reason that Japan has almost zero oil resources. Electronics were next, when Asian exporters made them a strategic priority. American companies moved abroad extensively, too, putting their labels on foreign-made products. Once consumers realized that their GE appliance, or even some Chrysler cars, were not actually made here, it became much easier to accept a host of other foreign-made products, and even to lose sight of where goods were manufactured altogether. "Who even knows what that means anymore?" became a pat response for those who couldn't be bothered to seek out American-made products.

At the same time those lines were blurring, the "Me Generation" began its ascendency. The philosophy that it was okay, even admirable, for a person to do what was in his or her own immediate best interests, regardless of the cost to his or her neighbors, customers, and others, took root. It was still possible for a customer to buy clothing, furniture, and other goods made within his or her own country, but fewer and fewer gave any thought to where their goods were coming from. When those shoppers walked into retail chains, they didn't think about the neighbor whose job might be cut because the store was no longer carrying goods made in his or her plant, or about the taxes his or her community would lose as unemployment increased and businesses shut down. Yes, the retailers have urged us into this apathetic emotional state, but we have allowed it. If enough of us insisted, the big chains would at least *feature* American-made products, just as they do organic products today.

For those of us who understand the importance of this issue, we become frustrated, and question why others don't care about the fate of their country, about the opportunities they and their friends and neighbors and children are losing. But, with limited exceptions, I don't really believe that most Americans are actively looking for foreign-made products. I also don't believe that most are considering the impact of their choices and opting to make those choices anyway. It is more that they do not think of it at all. That sounds sad and discouraging, but in fact it is great news. If people are not truly apathetic, if they truly haven't hardened their hearts to the damage caused by the choices they make, if they're not consciously putting money ahead of the future of this once-great country, we can educate them. Once they understand the difference they can make, they will—we can hope—be with us. We must reach out to as many people as possible and educate them about how each of us can make a significant difference. (I'll address strategies for doing so in more detail in Part III.)

I spent many years climbing the corporate ladder, and I saw firsthand that our own business leaders and the corporations they run have forgotten that they are Americans first. Comparing Panasonic of Japan to GE, our once great American electronics maker, is a sad lesson in national pride. Panasonic, Sony, Toshiba, Hitachi, NEC: These great companies of Japan never forgot that they are Japanese first. Yes, some of the cheapest stuff they sell in the USA is assembled in some third-world nations, but the key components are made, and the R&D, engineering, design, and manufacturing of the high-end products take place in their homeland. Our business leaders need to remember that they are Americans first. GE, especially under the pathetic leadership of Jack Welch, turned into a finance company that would rather issue a credit card than make stuff in the USA. Much of the manufacturing it still does has been shifted to places like Mexico. Whirlpool is still an American company making many appliances here, whereas GE has mostly sold us out.

Unlike executives from most other nations, many American businesspeople started to think of themselves and internationalists instead of Americans. That same perspective infiltrated Wall Street. Loyalty to a nation became a quaint and relatively insignificant concept, like favoring one sports team over another. Certainly, it should never rise to a level at which it would interfere with their way of doing business. Of course, when those same businesspeople and financiers needed a bailout, they suddenly remembered that they were Americans.

I understand how so many people were lulled into thinking this way. To some degree, in my youth, I myself was guilty of this ignorance. These free-trade falsehoods were offered up as fact in college, and it was not until I actually lived in Asia and kept coming face to face with the facts that I started to wake up. Fortunately, I know change is possible, and I'll share my personal observations on this point later in the book.

We need patriotic leadership in our business organizations again. Internationalists are tools: the unwitting tools of our downfall. Washington and our potential resurgence are also key factors in our downfall. Unfortunately, it is also the most contrived. The two-party system allows meaningful dissent only through one or both of the parties, but effectively stymies breakthroughs by even well-organized third-party efforts. The last time a new group really came to power was when the Republicans emerged as the party to free the slaves in the 1850s. Even then, the change did not occur in a vacuum; the

Republican ascent didn't create a three-party system or an open system. The Republican Party rose as the Whigs were declining, and stepped into what was tantamount to a vacant seat. There have been other efforts that gained some traction, like Theodore Roosevelt's Bull Moose Party and Ross Perot's toils, but none that were able to crack the power grip of the two parties in control. That does not appear changeable in the next few decades.

Washington, which should be part of the solution, has unfortunately botched it on so many levels. Politicians have failed to look out for the USA first; failed to assure that we have something close to a level playing field on wages, pollution, and other costs; failed to protect us from unsafe foreign products, including tens of millions of toys containing dangerous levels of lead and other chemicals; and borrowed far more than future generations can ever pay back, pushing us to the edge of insolvency. They do not have a real trade plan for goods or for energy. That said, there are members of both parties sympathetic to our cause. We need to lobby them at every opportunity, to try to cancel out the power of the big retail chains and foreigners.

It used to be that men and women served their country in politics from a sense of national duty. Today, it seems as if those who want to be politicians crave the façade of power. We must hold them much more accountable. Just like the retailers discussed earlier, politicians are susceptible to pressure from those who keep them where they want to be. For the retailers, that means in a profitable business position; for the politicians, it means in office. In both cases, the concept is the same: When we let them know that they must address this problem if they want our continued business (or votes), we'll get their attention.

Washington presents an obstacle to fixing this situation, but it's not an insurmountable one. We can and will make America great again. Looking at the problem and the bad decisions that brought us to this point can be discouraging, but stick with me. The shackles on our industrial economy can be broken. All five of the problems that caused our industrial economy to decay can be solved if we just join together and take a firm stand.

Chapter 3 The Energy Deficit Is Solvable

There's more. We are facing not one, but two massive deficits: the trade deficit for goods, as discussed in the previous chapter, and a deficit for imported energy that is nearly as dramatic (see Figures 3.1 through 3.4).

I've already established that our nation's economic survival is at stake. Our wealth is being sapped from our nation at rates unprecedented in nonwartime history. No country or empire to date has survived such a significant transfer of its wealth to other nations. Like an individual or a company, a nation cannot mathematically outspend its income forever. The energy deficit is about oil and, to a lesser degree, natural gas. The United States was the site of the first oil boom, and many subsequent, starting in Pennsylvania and moving into Texas, Oklahoma, California, and Alaska. Our energy was exported all over the world, and helped us win two world wars.

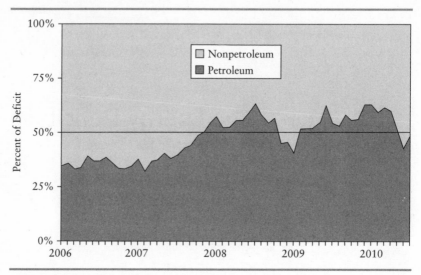

FIGURE 3.1 Petroleum versus Nonpetroleum as Percent of U.S. Goods and Services Trade Deficit

Source: U.S. Census Bureau: www.census.gov/foreign-trade/statistics/graphs/PetroleumImports.html.

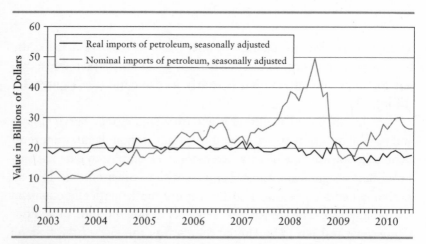

FIGURE 3.2 Comparison of Nominal and Real (Chain-Weighted) Imports of Petroleum

Source: U.S. Census Bureau: www.census.gov/foreign-trade/statistics/graphs/PetroleumImports.html.

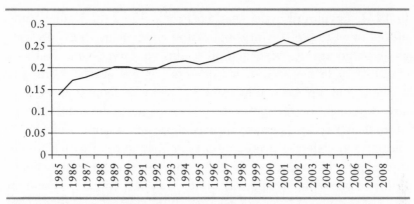

FIGURE 3.3   Percentage of Foreign Petroleum of Total U.S. Energy Consumption
Source: U.S. Census Bureau: www.census.gov/foreign-trade/statistics/graphs/PetroleumImports.html.

Today we have a massive petroleum deficit; between $20 and $30 billion is being drained from our economy every month.[1] Imported carbon-based energy, namely oil, is now our enemy. The energy crisis is not new. We have left behind decades of missed opportunities. Many of us have personally experienced our vulnerability to foreign oil, since the Organization of the Petroleum Exporting Countries (OPEC) initially stuck it to us in the energy shock in the 1970s.

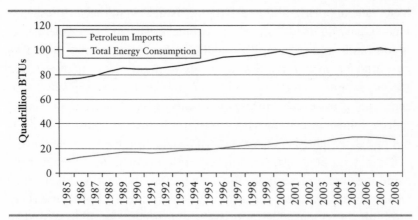

FIGURE 3.4   Total U.S. Energy Used versus Foreign Petroleum
Source: U.S. Census Bureau: www.census.gov/foreign-trade/statistics/graphs/PetroleumImports.html.

In 1973, Egypt and Syria attacked Israel. When the United States moved to assist Israel with supplies and equipment, OPEC declared an embargo against exporting oil to this country. I remember as a child sitting in the back of my parents' big gas guzzler waiting in a long line to buy gas and listening to them talk about how we were now dependent on foreigners for oil—foreigners who didn't like us. More than 30 years later, we are even more dependent on foreign oil, and have transferred a mountain of money abroad to pay for it. I remember the urgency of the time, and how it exposed the vulnerability of our economy and way of life. To our detriment, we let that sense of urgency fade away over time. Instead of telling OPEC what they could do with their oil, and then re-creating and reinventing our energy usage and production capabilities, we have sat around for all these years, letting chances to address the problem slip through our fingers.

The new, large oil fields are mostly abroad, many in countries that actively oppose freedom, like Venezuela, Iran, and Saudi Arabia. Each opposes basic freedoms we in this country take for granted. Saudi Arabia's prodigious financial support of radical Islamic schools throughout the region has been a root cause in the spread of those willing to attack the West. The Saudi government may not support terrorists directly, but some of that oil money is definitely ending up with them. Iran is actively working on nuclear weapons, and their leaders have talked openly about destroying Israel. Venezuela's president, Hugo Chavez, intends to be the next Fidel Castro in Latin America; he is constantly and very vocally making up for some personal deficiency by attacking the United States, in my opinion. Each of these three nations suppresses the basic rights and human dignities of its own citizens, jailing and even torturing opponents. Being dependent on them—indeed, allowing them to have a huge trade surplus because of oil—is not just shortsighted and weak-willed on our part, but it's dangerous.

Time is running out, yes, but we can do something about it if we stand together and act now. We have to grab the energy deficit problem by the horns *today* and attack it on multiple levels, because there are both short- and long-term issues that need to be addressed. The good news is that with enough will and follow-through, the problem is truly solvable. Those solutions, if implemented, will have the added benefit of restoring thousands of jobs.

HEROES OF OUR USA EFFORT IN THEIR OWN WORDS

America's True Athletic Clothing Maker: Wickers

There was a time when America produced what its citizens needed and wanted. We were proud to have abundant natural resources and dedicated people to do this. Today, we have squandered our ability to use these resources, and put ourselves in the position of having to depend on others.

We have lost our pride! We are losing our self-confidence, as well, to believe that we can regain what we have squandered.

Near 10 percent unemployment, about 30 million people not working: Is this a lasting legacy of the movement of manufacturing and farm products to low-wage countries? What is the new norm but a euphemism for "not to expect that we will return to our previous grandeur; to settle for less"? Is the American dream gone forever?

It doesn't have to be.

There is a real "food movement" starting in America, for example. Its objective is to set the path away from the multi-international corporations, the food preparation industries, and the fast-food companies that have created an unhealthy diet (which has contributed to an increase in the number of illnesses such as Type-2 Diabetes, heart diseases, and some forms of cancers in the American populations), toward a more sustainable and healthy food chain that is closer to local farms and farmers' market distributors.

The idea of the movement is that we can do better than what is being done now; it's also a prima facie case for all manufacturing and distribution: We *can* get our pride back and build a better America by getting back to our roots.

Small businesses do not move away to distant lands to produce products; they stay and compete. Large corporations have built well-known brands in America, then moved away to produce what they sell in America. What they don't know is that, in doing so, they also take our pride from all of us. Not only have the skills of factory workers deteriorated, but also the knowledge of our research scientists and information technology professionals, and, increasingly, the creative aspirations of our young people.

Loss of our pride can easily be seen when an unshackled financial industry can reap billions and cause a debacle that affects all of us more than it does them. The food movement needs to morph into a total reversing movement if we are to regain our pride by doing what made us great to begin with. Grow our own food, build our own products in our own factories, and allow our young people to have the opportunity to utilize the creative genius that still exists in America.

(continued)

(*continued*)

To understand fully the impact of the transferring of our industrial legacy, one must view the total devastation of fiber, textile, and apparel manufacturing in the United States.

America was the world leader in the production of synthetic fibers; since the 1930s, we had the premier researchers and developers of innovative uses of these fibers. Billions of pounds of fibers were manufactured in the United States, providing employment for not only the factory workers and managers, but also for the many thousands employed to seek new markets and build consumer demand in the textile markets for home furnishings, apparel, automotive interiors, tires, ecosystems, and many other end-use products.

All the science, technology, and manufacturing know-how is now gone from our shores. They are now closer to their direct customers in textiles production. The textile industries' production of yarn spinning, fabric formations, dyeing, and finishing skills, with its attendant technology to create fabrics to meet the needs of the American consumer, and that employed thousands of skilled workers in their factories have moved; forced to do so by the market forces and a system created by the political fantasy that it would be best for U.S. citizens.

This political fantasy, that apparel manufacturing would be best if it also moved to low-wage producing lands, pulled not only manufacturing but also the largest retailers in the world to set up their procurement departments in these same low-wage producing countries. That meant hundreds of thousands of garment workers were no longer needed by these factories in America. Many of the total number of U.S. citizens formerly employed by these industries are now among the 30 million unemployed or underemployed Americans.

We have been told that this giveaway of America's manufacturing prowess, believed to have been the finest in the world, and which delivered the goods to help our armed forces defeat the totalitarian regimes 60 years ago, and then to help build the greatest middle class known to mankind, is now but a shell of its former self. To be replaced by what? Do you know, or can you see, what our political establishment vision is?

We want our collective pride back!

Japan is a nation sorely lacking in domestic sources of energy, and living there was an awakening for me. The country has almost no oil and just a bit of coal. That left it little choice but to build cars with energy efficiency as a top priority; that priority is backed up in government regulation and tax policy favoring the purchase of fuel-efficient cars. The Japanese also have an extensive nuclear power system, which has saved them hundreds of billions of dollars in imported oil over the years. They also cleverly harness water power by using periods of excess nuclear energy availability late at night to pump water to reservoirs in the mountains, thereby letting gravity generate more electricity during peak times as the water runs back through dams. Their hydroelectric efforts would not be nearly so effective most of the year without this boost from nuclear power. Energy has always been a national strategic priority in Japan. We must make it a top priority in the United States, too.

If we could galvanize our people to think in terms of the patriotic urgency of saving energy, we could pursue the immediate and long-terms goals to make a real difference, today and tomorrow. Our nation demonstrated this resolve and determination during World War II, and we can do so again. Instead of planting victory gardens, we can reduce energy consumption—immediately. Businesses, organizations, and individuals can and must cut waste and seek out ways to increase efficiency. We can pursue locally produced green energy, like biodiesel fuels; make smarter use of our existing electricity grid; introduce efficiency upgrades to existing power plants; increase local production of solar, wind, and electric cars; raise the number of longer-term new, safe, secure, locally produced nuclear power plants; and actively investigate other strategies and devices to reduce consumption and produce energy in the USA. In order to implement these massive changes, however, we need an injection of new energy and excitement—the kind of energy and excitement that accompanied the lunar program in the 1960s. That's the level of urgency and motivation we'll need if we're to substantially replace carbon-based energy over the next two decades. The solution might be fusion, hydrogen, ultraefficient solar, or something beyond our present imagination. Whatever the ultimate answer, the first step is to make the decision to prioritize finding that solution.

That said, the most immediate and best investment in reducing foreign energy imports is not developing a new source, but improving our efficiency so that we use less. This goes for both individuals and businesses. Many simple steps that require little or no money up front and a relatively small effort can have a major impact over time. These steps all begin with being conscious of the need to conserve energy, avoiding waste, and becoming more energy-efficient all-around. Just as many Americans buy foreign-made goods, thereby perpetuating the trade deficit and all the ills it brings, without ever considering the consequences of their actions, many Americans miss everyday opportunities to cut back on their energy usage. For example, if a family has two cars, they can choose the more fuel-efficient one more often, especially taking it on longer drives, leaving the gas guzzler home. Turning off lights and appliances when not in use, and unplugging power adapters that continuously sap electricity, may seem like insignificant actions, but those small savings add up when multiplied across thousands in this country who make energy-conscious choices.

Other efforts do require a little money up front. I use a push reel mower that uses zero gas; it is made by Indiana-based American Lawn Mowers, which has been in business since 1895.[2] Next time you buy a car or truck, make fuel efficiency one of your top priorities, along with choosing one made in the USA. My Ford Escape hybrid easily gets 31.5 miles to the gallon in overall daily driving; and if I lay off the gas pedal a little bit, I can easily get it up over 35 miles per gallon. Becoming more energy-efficient not only deprives foreign powers of our money, it has the added benefit of putting real money back into our pockets and keeping the environment cleaner. Such a deal!

Business and government can also have a marked impact, and may find that they are able to save money while helping us get out from under energy imports. From the smallest to the biggest business, it is time to take a look and see what can be saved. In the summer, my local post office has its air conditioner set so cold that the employees are wearing sweaters, though it's 90 degrees outside. Easing up on the air conditioning would save energy and, apparently, would make the staff a bit more comfortable. Again, the savings from that specific change might be relatively small, but what if every business and governmental office across the country turned their air conditioners up a couple of degrees? The bigger the business, the bigger the potential savings. I completely understand how one can get busy at work and put issues like power consumption on the back burner, so to speak, but it is time for businesses across the country to form power-savings teams, whose members gauge, analyze, and have the authority to make changes in the name of energy savings. I also am fully aware that each and every busy businessperson and factory worker probably has 80 to-do items already on his or her list, but I guarantee that you and your management will be favorably impressed with the savings for your company if you give power usage some real attention. Plus, you will be doing your patriotic duty for our country by reducing foreign energy imports!

Another positive effect of reduced energy use is decreased pollution. No matter what we think about global warming, we can all agree that breathing in less pollution is a good thing for our children—for all of us. When I moved from a town in the Midwest to California, I remember being shocked by the high levels of smog and the air pollution. I also recall the regularly issued smog pollution warnings, alerting parents to bring their kids inside. I can't even say when the last such smog warning was posted, but it has been years since I noticed a problem. What made the difference? Better engines have made our cars burn fuels more cleanly, and coupled with changed attitudes, we have already made a big head start on reducing oil consumption.

Another positive effect of using less oil is that it takes just a small reduction in usage of any commodity to cause a meaningful drop in market prices. In one of my roles at Western Digital, I oversaw market research. The effect of slight changes in supply and demand on market pricing was a key point in my research and analysis, and I found that plus or minus less than 3 percent of supply to natural demand was sufficient to prompt very large swings in market pricing. Too much supply by over 3 percent, and the market price drops off a cliff. Not enough supply by 3 percent, and the prices shoot up, as buyers bid up pricing to keep their factories running. With regard to energy, the price shift caused by even a modest cut in consumption will leave surplus on the market, because oil wells cannot be shut off like a light switch. The excess will quickly force prices down. The challenge for us is to stay vigilant about reduced energy consumption on an ongoing basis, even if prices fall in the short term. Prices will rise again in the future if we do not continue to lower consumption, and certainly the problem will not be solved if we ignore it. That is what happened in the late 1970s. Gas prices went back down and folks went back to using as much as ever, eventually forcing demand and prices back up. This time has to be different. We must keep our eye on the ball and end our dependence on foreign energy, no matter what happens to the price of gas in the short term.

Instead of investing in *safer* upgraded nuclear technology, as in France, Sweden, and Japan, we allowed a few Hollywood movies to scare us, and effectively push us into the arms of the Arabs by largely ignoring nuclear energy development for two decades. Even minimal progress in increasing output from existing nuclear plants, and strategically adding just a few more plants would have cut pollution emissions into the air by millions of metric tons, compared with the carbon-burning power plants we still rely on. And, of course, our energy import needs could have been substantially reduced. We need to pursue a plan that includes ultrasafe nuclear power, which will also create hundreds of thousands of good construction jobs.

Effectively tackling the energy challenge overall would produce millions of jobs—real jobs, not contrived government statistics. For example, upgrading or building 500 power plants across our country would create 1 million good construction jobs, assuming 2,000 jobs per project. Those projects would also benefit millions of other workers who provide support, such as concrete and steel production and delivery, engineering, and others. Updating our power grid would employ many additional tens of thousands in good-paying jobs. This is stimulus that really works, creating jobs and wealth that benefit the country by directly abating our dependence on foreign energy. Those billions of dollars would be recycled here in the USA, generating even more prosperity at home. Talk about stimulus!

Solar and wind technologies, which have been practically ignored until relatively recently, account for only a tiny fraction of power generation in this country. Clean, cheap, and absolutely renewable, these should have been a strategic objective of the government since the 1970s, at least on a par with the moon shot. We should have been leading the world in these industries; instead, we find ourselves scrambling to buy solar and wind power equipment from abroad. It is vital to keep in mind that "green jobs" will become available here only if we actually make the solar panels and wind turbines in the USA. Importing this equipment from China while talking about green jobs here in the USA is a cruel irony for those folks in the unemployment line. The nurturing of these industries in this country must be a strategic priority, as it is in China; and they must be protected from foreigners dumping their solar panels and other equipment on our market. Our future security depends on it.

Keep in mind, the key oil-producing nations are not just against democracy; they are police states. Anyone who openly criticizes their government risks arrest, and worse. These are the powers where our energy dollars flow. What would happen if there were a larger war that might involve them? Would this foreign energy continue to flow? Or would they leave our economy crippled, by joining the other side against us? The fact is, we are very vulnerable to a supply cutoff situation.

Oil money has directly or indirectly funded terrorism, yet we have spent more than a trillion dollars on the second Iraq war and occupation. What if we had spent just 10 percent of that money on cutting back foreign energy consumption? By reducing our reliance on foreign oil, we take money out of the pockets of those who would fund terror against us. Remember, by reducing oil consumption, we neuter the ability of a Chavez to run amuck. The same is true with nations like China, which produce so much for us but do not respect basic freedoms. We are supporting the efforts of such countries to become greater world powers. When we have some trade with them on an equal footing, we have influence. When we are completely dependent on them for cheap goods, they influence us. Don't believe they are influencing us today? It hasn't been so long since we held our heads high and told nations we did not support where they could take their trade. Could you see us trading with Stalin or Hitler? No way! Those are extreme examples, but today the blacklist of nations we will not trade with has shrunk dramatically, to nasty nations that do not have anything we want anyway. North Korea has nothing we want—now. But if the North Koreans suddenly discovered the largest pool of oil outside Saudi Arabia, probably it would not take long for us to start dealing with them. We used to stand as a shining light of freedom and democracy, to inspire the world. Today, we will take a righteous tone only with a country that has nothing of value to offer us. Our leadership as a nation no longer rings true; and it shows. No wonder our influence around the globe is on the wane.

As long and harsh as the energy deficit has been, it can probably be affected more apparently in the immediate term through a combination of science and relatively minor changes in consumer behavior. If we treat it like the emergency it is, and act accordingly, we can attack it head-on and win this fight. Look at the amazing technological changes that were accomplished during World War II. We need real energy if we are to provide real solutions; the men and women who work toward these solutions, whether scientists in labs or entrepreneurs in their garages, will be the heroes of our future. The spirit that motivates them is America's greatest asset. Together, without a doubt, we can solve the energy deficit.

We're faced with two very serious problems: the trade deficit, with regard to goods, and the energy deficit. The good news is that just as the problems are intertwined, so are the solutions. Working to reduce our dependence on foreign oil will also go a long way toward achieving our goals to restore jobs, retool manufacturing, and put our industry back in a position to compete with any nation in the world. Once the ball is rolling, recovery will gather momentum, just as the decline has. Let's get behind that ball together and give it a good push, right now.

It can and will be done if you are with me and take the stand.

Chapter 4 Dispelling the Service Economy Myth

Deindustrialization Means Fewer Jobs, Lower Pay, and Less Opportunity

For years the media has been telling us not to worry about factories closing. Everything will be rosy, they tell us, as our manufacturing economy turns into a "service economy." This was a blatant falsehood on a number of levels, one that has become increasingly apparent, for four reasons: (1) Service industry jobs have failed to appear in the numbers needed to replace manufacturing; (2) they typically pay much less than manufacturing jobs; (3) they are easier to eliminate; and (4) mathematically, they add much less value to our economy than manufacturing jobs.

This is not to say that service jobs don't play an important role in our society; they do. Nor am I minimizing the contribution of those who hold them. But in strictly economic terms, they simply do not add as much value as manufacturing jobs. According to the U.S. Bureau of Labor Statistics, the average goods-producing (manufacturing) job today pays $32.59 an hour, versus $16.20 in the service industry, including the cost of benefits.[1] That means manufacturing jobs pay, on average across our nation, including all benefits, twice what service jobs do. It gets worse from there.

The higher-paying service economy jobs, like a being a lawyer or a pharmacist, make up only a small percentage of the total. The vast majority of service jobs are in retail or food service, at much lower rates of pay than manufacturing, and few, if any, benefits. Once upon a time, young people took this sort of service job part-time to gain experience or to help them pay for school. Now, college graduates are accepting these positions as their only alternative. Most service jobs for young people are one-way tickets to joining the working poor. Many borrowed money to go to college and could owe as much as $50,000, or even twice that.

As jobs that require the skills and knowledge acquired while earning most college degrees continue to disappear, in greater numbers these young people will end up in service jobs that don't even require a high school education. Some college graduates are, literally, pouring coffee. Good, desirable service jobs exist because of manufacturing. For example, manufacturers employ mainly those who are involved directly or indirectly in the manufacturing process; but they also need higher-paid service employees, like accountants, engineers, and lawyers. I, myself, held a number of service roles over the years for a manufacturer, in both finance and marketing. Such roles enable a company to sell its items, inform potential customers about what is available, develop new products, deal with employment issues, make sure everyone is paid, and so on. Because a factory exists, a host of jobs beyond the actual manufacturing process are created and supported.

Replacing every manufacturing industry job lost with a service industry job is wildly unrealistic; and even if it were possible, it wouldn't solve the problem. It would actually take many more service industry jobs to restore an economy to the strength of its manufacturing days, since, as just noted, they typically offer lower wages.

HEROES OF OUR USA EFFORT IN THEIR OWN WORDS

The Denim Tradition Keeper: Texas Jeans

Nearly all of the jean manufacturers have left the United States, to be sewn in foreign countries. Not only has this hurt the customer with inferior quality, it has contributed to a dramatic decrease in the number of jobs in this country and the strength of American manufacturing.

We support more than 300 employees in our community and give them a sense of support. We manufacture a premium-quality product—maintaining high standards of quality, fit, and customer service—right here in the United States. We prove that American manufacturing can still mean something real. We think a lot of people are going to find it well worth it to get a high-quality product that not only fits right, but that also helps keep jobs in our country.

There are a lot of people looking for work in this country. They don't have the education to be a doctor or a lawyer, but they want to put in an honest day's work to be able to support themselves and their families. The American worker really wants to make a quality product they can be proud of.

Americans were once a leading force in the world's manufacturing economy. We built things to last and be proud of. That spirit has never gone away in workers, even though "big business" has abandoned them for offshore profits. An American worker will give you his or her all, knowing he or she is making something that he or she can be proud of.

Over the past five years we have occasionally thought about closing or selling the business. However, particularly since 9/11, we feel an obligation to do what we can to offer my employees work, and try to do my part to maintain the made-in-America manufacturing tradition that made this country strong. Texas Jeans is continuing to grow. Who knows, maybe one day you will see them all over. If you do, you can be sure that they've been made in the USA.

For example, if your region loses one million manufacturing jobs at which workers are paid $60,000 annually, with benefits and overtime, how many service economy jobs would it need to add just to break even? Assuming very generously that the service economy wages average $40,000 per year with benefits, and that one million service industry jobs were added, those lost manufacturing jobs would drain $60 billion from that economy, and only $40 billion would be added back. In this scenario, even if the net job loss were zero, the region would be $20 billion worse off. At these wage estimates, 1.5 million service jobs would be needed just to make up for the overall economic loss of the manufacturing jobs.

Even at that painful breakeven point, however, all is still not equal. An economy that grows at a slower rate than the population is, in fact, shrinking. And those service workers and their children are still going to need an education and other government services. Three workers making $40,000 a year typically pay much less in taxes than two who make $60,000. Local governments will see tax revenues drop just when they need more resources.

Most importantly, even if 50 percent more service jobs were created than manufacturing jobs were lost, those new workers would still lack disposable income. A manufacturing worker earning $60,000 per year has much more disposable income than the service worker making $40,000 per year. The service economy gives rise to a new class of working poor, who are unable to pay off student loans, make a down payment on a home, build up a nest egg for retirement, or improve their financial positions in any significant way. Many do not even get the benefits that most of us consider basic.

In reality, this hypothetical is overly optimistic. Many service jobs pay $10 an hour or less and offer no benefits. Wal-Mart is now our country's largest employer, and many of the company's associates make barely more than minimum wage and have no benefits. How can they get by?

The economic multiplier effect discussed in Chapter 1 is responsible for the generation of a great deal of positive economic activity. Service economy activity generates much less ancillary activity than manufacturing. This just makes sense mathematically, as manufacturing activity needs a constant source of supplies and support. Service occupations, like the practice of law, need very little in the way of supplies or outside support, relative to manufacturing requirements. In short, the multiplier is a lot higher for manufacturing activities than for service activities: about 1.7 for manufacturing versus 1.2 for service activities. So while every dollar spent on manufacturing here in the USA generates about $1.70 in positive economic activity, service spending of the same dollar generates only about $1.20.

Because of the much lower economic multiplier effect, replacement of manufacturing jobs with service industry jobs would be a disaster for a local community, even if lost wages were restored in full. Imagine that a factory in Springfield, Illinois, closes, eliminating jobs worth $10 million; yet, at same time, the local government manages to snare a credit card phone service center that has jobs also worth $10 million in local economic activity. Because of the very different nature of these jobs and the lower multiplier effect, the service jobs generate only $12 million in local economic activity, far from the $17 million the manufacturing jobs were generating. That $5 million drop in economic activity in that community translates directly into fewer jobs, lower tax revenues, and fewer opportunities for its people. Service jobs have their place, of course, but they will never take the place of real manufacturing jobs.

In my years in corporate finance, I saw firsthand that service jobs are much easier to eliminate in the short run than manufacturing jobs. There is a lot of money tied up in a factory, and the finance department does not want it idle—unless, of course, it does not produce sufficiently to cover variable costs. (*Variable cost* is the actual material cost of the item produced plus the cost of labor to produce it.) As long as a factory makes more money than the total cost of materials and labor, managing for positive cash flow dictates it should remain open. Furthermore, it is expensive to shutter a factory, and can take months or even years of planning and action to close it down completely. Service jobs can be eliminated virtually overnight. In some cases, it is simply a matter of sending out notices, as opposed to the huge amount of work involved in closing a factory.

How long does it take to terminate a service-related job versus one in manufacturing? Most service jobs can be eliminated immediately or, at most, within two weeks. Moreover, a sizable percentage of service jobs can be performed by any other minimally skilled worker, with the exception of a few areas, like the medical and legal fields. Even much legal work can be outsourced to places like India. In contrast, a factory can cut back on the total number of workers by slowing down production and reducing the number of shifts, but the investment in capital equipment behooves the company to keep it running to some degree, or risk losing the workforce that can run and maintain the machinery. That is changing now.

Recently, entire factories are being closed, to be outsourced to China or other low-wage countries. Although this is still an expensive process, the costs quoted by Chinese contractors are so exceedingly low that companies are gutting factories and sending equipment abroad. The Chinese government really wants those manufacturing jobs.

Yes, many service jobs are appropriate and important for our economy, in particular in fields such as nursing and teaching; but is it really necessary for 500,000 Californians, roughly 1 in 50 adults,[2] to have their real estate sales licenses? This situation shows how the "higher-paid" service jobs sprout like mushrooms during economic good times, then are vaporized as soon as the economy turns downward. During the housing boom, real estate agents proliferated. A real estate agent I know works in an office that supported 30 people two years ago; now it is down to 6—and many who remain are making a tiny fraction of what they were just a few years ago. Their situation is not unusual.

During the housing bubble, my wife and I realized it was time to switch from owning to renting. I was approached by real estate agents in many guises, including a florist, a cashier at the grocery store, a secretary at work, and others. It seemed like the whole world wanted to help service (read: pressure) us, and offered up reason after reason that housing prices would keep shooting up.

"House prices never drop," one assured me.

"They did in 1989," I said.

"Oh, you know that? It was a special circumstance . . . [blah, blah, blah]."

"Prices were up over 20 percent last year, and you are going to miss out," another warned.

"Is that sustainable?" I asked. He nodded vigorously.

"Well, at that rate, no new owners can possibly afford to buy, which means the market is not mathematically sustainable, right?"

"Math *what*?" he asked.

My favorite was the default argument: "Those immigrants are still buying, and are going to drive up prices."

To this, I'd countered: "You mean they are just aching to cross the border and spend $600,000 on a house?"

The response to this was nearly always the fervent *yes*! of the true believer.

Worse than not adding value to our society, some of those service jobs were actually a drag on our prosperity. The same folks who created all sorts of myths about real estate, which helped to push prices into the stratosphere, were always the ones to act shocked when prices went over a cliff. In the end, did all their paper-pushing add any value to society, or take a bitter toll?

There are, of course, really good-paying service jobs. For example, let's say the town where I live adds another divorce attorney. Good-paying service job, right, so we should be happy? Now let's say the community has just enough divorce attorneys. In such a case, they might tend to encourage couples to get marriage counseling, see their minister, or take time to reconsider. However, if new ones keep coming to town, accelerating competition for the same pool of clients, eventually there will be less marriage counseling and more divorces. I watched in high school as my parents divorced, with their lawyers spurring them on. Savings and dreams destroyed, a married couple soon becomes two much poorer single people. There is a threshold of necessity, but beyond that what value is added to society by the creation of additional positions?

Making something in a factory, building a home, and creating the things we need to live our everyday lives all add real value to our society. There was no shelter on that land, and a family built a home there, so now they are better off.

Can we find an example of a state here in this country that actually runs on a service economy? Probably the best example is Florida, with its huge tourist trade and large retiree population. Florida benefits from tens of millions of tourists bringing their savings and credit cards to spend in the Sunshine State; and millions of retirees bring their life savings, plus the pensions they earned working somewhere else. This stimulates a viable economy, but only as long as there is a constant flow of tourists and retirees. The service jobs are in restaurants, retail, and some in health care. The first two types of businesses are low-paying, and can close at a moment's notice. The third does offer some good-paying jobs, but they represent a tiny fraction of the overall total. When trends change and people go elsewhere, spend less, or retire later—meaning, in this case, spending less money in Florida—how will the service economy sustain itself? It won't. It will shrink in a matter of months.

Unlike manufacturing-based economies that spark the growth of other industries, service-related work just disappears when the restaurant or store closes. Not going to happen? This "new economy" is already causing people to completely rethink retirement. Large numbers working a few more years translates into hundreds of millions of dollars less spent in the retirement meccas of Florida. Additionally, the pensions the retirees used to bring with them might be less in the future, and more retirees will be showing up with no pension at all. Many could choose to stay in the family home a few years longer after retirement, even if they are not working, to add to their nest egg and be closer to family. States and communities that count on their service economies are at the mercy of wealth transfers via tourism or retirees. This model is going up in smoke, and with it a key success element in the service economy myth.

Drawing on the U.S. Bureau of Labor Statistics data showing the contrast between manufacturing and service industry wages and benefits, it is hard to imagine that anyone could believe that replacing manufacturing facilities with service ones, like resorts or hotels, makes sense. To fully understand the difference between service industry jobs and manufacturing jobs, consider the varying impacts of a new hotel opening in an area, versus a new factory. The workers at the factory would be earning $30, $40, maybe $50 an hour on overtime, versus the hotel workers making just over minimum wage. The factory would use steel from our nation, and hundreds of other components made all over the country. The hotel would consume some food supplies for its guests, but the total would be just a fraction of the amount of supplies required by the factory. The workers at the factory would draw on years of experience, like master craftsmen. Some would learn tooling skills, the highly advanced ability to make the tools that keep the machines running. The hotel workers would get some training, true, and no doubt take pride in their work. But the vast majority of the hotel's employees would be, essentially, interchangeable; hired and fired from season to season. Few hotel workers are ever given much formal training by their employers, as they are expected to be able to perform their basic tasks when they walk in the door. It is crystal clear which type of job would add greater economic value for both the workers and the community.

The service economy overall is dependent on value added by manufacturing jobs. We can only serve those who have the means to stay in the hotel, purchase the cup of coffee, or hire someone to walk their dogs. More taxes are drawn off the higher economic activity manu-facturing work. Every time a major manufacturing plant moves over-seas, a local economy suffers, even when it receives aid from the state or federal government. Many communities that have lost factories and cannot make ends meet are now turning in desperation to the ultimate service economy dream tax: casinos. Entertainment is all well and good; even I like to go to a casino occasionally. However, these facilities—and lotteries for that matter—are feeding off the 1 percent of the population that easily becomes addicted to gambling. Much like alcoholics, habitual gamblers cannot control their behavior the way most people can. Having a casino nearby is a constant, and dangerous, attraction to them. They and their families pay the price for these desperate attempts by government to fill budget holes. And still the holes remain.

When a factory is built—something that rarely happens in the United States anymore—service jobs suddenly spring up all over that community to provide services to the factory and its employees. Res-taurants and shops open; the school district hires teachers; soon there is another dentist, doctor, and hair salon. All because the factory opened, offering good wages and purchasing from local suppliers.

Does a casino prompt the same sort of economic activity? There is an initial spurt of economic activity when the construction companies are building the facility. But it's the equivalent of a sugar high for the community, as the millions that were borrowed to build the casino are spent there. When the doors open, however, those good construc-tion jobs go away, and the casino hires mostly low-wage service employees. That in itself is not such a bad thing, except that the com-munity does not get the ongoing boost it would from a factory, because of the low wages and the lower economic multiplier. In fact, the casino is sucking wealth out of the community and others within a drivable range. In the end, most of that money does not stay in the community. It gets sent to the casino company's headquarters. Replacing factory jobs with blackjack dealer or waitress jobs leaves the community much poorer.

The same could be said for service jobs in a shopping strip mall, versus a traditional downtown shopping area. There is nothing at all wrong with the folks doing these jobs, but traditional downtowns do a lot more good locally. Local governments often give aggressive tax breaks to these malls in the mistaken belief that there is an inordinately large economic benefit to having a new strip of storefronts. As with the casino, the community gets a boost as the buildings are being constructed, but soon thereafter finds that the vast majority of the jobs created are low-paying retail types, and none of the profits stay in town. The local city council members shake their heads when they see the result of having spent millions to woo the developer; still, they believe they can at least claim victory from the sales tax they collect. In reality, they have to balance those sales tax gains against the reduction in sales tax generated by the locally owned shops, which will have a very hard time competing with the large chain stores in the strip mall. Plus, most of the money earned by locally owned retailers stays local, whereas most of the revenue from the chain stores at the new strip mall leaves the community. Local retailers have a real stake in that community, professional and personal, and it shows. Not the case over at the strip mall. The original financial estimates almost never take into account the resources the city will have to expend to support the strip mall in the form of roads, police, and other services. Eventually, the big chain stores put the local retailers out of business; crime prevention becomes more expensive, due to the increasing number of vacant shops; and available jobs are those on the lowest rung on the ladder.

Almost any community would be far better off simply by dedicating a much smaller amount of resources to making sure local merchants stay healthy. A service economy means more people working harder but earning less. We get poorer as a nation by going in this direction. We need to recognize that although we do need service jobs, they cannot replace good-paying manufacturing jobs. The economic value of service jobs is naturally much lower to the local, state, and even national economy. The pay is lower, too. And the ability to eliminate them is almost immediate. Remember, service jobs are dependent on manufacturing jobs or an influx of outside money, such as from tourists or retirees. Most problematic, the economic multiplier factor of service jobs is so much lower than that of manufacturing jobs that, all else being equal, they leave communities much worse off financially.

Bottom line: We still need factories. We must rebuild American manufacturing.

Chapter 5 Economic Judgment Day

We have choices to make in the very near future that will either renew our nation and push it to new heights, or keep us on the path to economic decay and ruin. Inaction is a choice that will ensure a dark future for all of us (see Figure 5.1).

We must decide to act, to restore jobs, retool industry, and compete head-on with the world; or we must accept defeat. This seems like an obvious choice, but apathy has grown deeply entrenched in our society over the past few decades. Apathy, or the lack of caring, has always been the ultimate enemy of freedom and democracy. Politicians often encourage this apathy in order to retain their power. Listening to their siren song is easier than making a conscious choice to be part of the solution.

Here is what excellence would mean for our future:

- Good jobs are abundant, and they pay more than enough to support a family.
- Local governments and school systems are not broke; they actually have the resources they need to build their communities and take care of their citizens, without having to borrow to make ends meet.
- Most of those who want to own homes can afford to do so—though perhaps not the McMansions of a few years ago.
- Parents welcome their new babies into the world with hope, instead of fearing for their future.
- When people think of the days ahead, they do so with optimism, not apprehension.
- A healthy pride about what we have accomplished, coupled with a positive feeling about what the future will bring, is almost universal.

Of course, we would still face problems as a nation and as a people, but these troubles would be challenges to overcome, not reasons to give up. People would generally feel secure in the knowledge that they are in charge and can make a real difference, personally and for their communities.

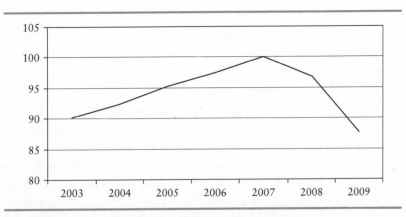

FIGURE 5.1 Total Manufacturing Activity Index
Source: Federal Reserve, www.federalreserve.gov/datadownload/
Download.aspx?rel=G17&series=a10b61b9a174694f9589c95345085
dfd&lastObs=7&from=&to=&filetype=csv&label=include&layout=
seriesrow&type=package.

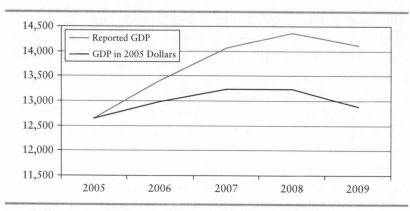

FIGURE 5.2   Real GDP Has Not Grown Since 2005
Source: Adapted from data by the Bureau of Economic Analysis.

Alternatively, if we continue down the road toward decline, bad economic and social times will get worse and worse (see Figure 5.2). Today's recessions would turn into tomorrow's depressions. Even when times were not so bad, there would be fewer and fewer good jobs to be found, and those available would pay much less than we are accustomed to today. Consumers, businesses, and even local and state governments would face economic chaos, and bankruptcy for all of these groups would abound. Many pension plans would collapse, and those that did remain would be cut back, paying much less than what folks were promised. Overall unemployment would rise, and could stay above 20 percent. The dollar would become practically worthless. Crime would become more and more commonplace. Neighborhoods everywhere, and even individuals, would be forced to pay for private security. Apathy would be on the rise, and escapism through drugs and alcohol would become the rule of the day. People would fear for the future and view it with dread. Parents would seriously consider not bringing children into this world.

Down this path, America's time would be over.

Pension funds that are already underfunded would be the first to go. Many of those currently reporting a moderately strong position might also turn out to be underfunded, as their projections are based on a 7 to 9 percent return on investment. In good times, this is no problem; but in bad times, those returns won't be forthcoming—in fact, they are completely unrealistic. The government entity charged with safeguarding pensions is itself considerably underfunded. This agency is paying only roughly 70 percent of previous pension payments for those funds that collapse today. According to the *Wall Street Journal*, total government pensions were underfunded by nearly $500 billion as of the end of 2009.[1]

Government in many cities and states and at the federal level has not been putting away enough money to pay for benefits promised to its employees. Underfunding a government pension is a dangerous gamble, which many of these entities are taking to reduce their required cash outlay today, with dramatic results in the future. If the economy continues to decay from deindustrialization and falling tax revenues (see Figure 5.3), desperate governmental bodies will have to try to raise taxes, and in so doing further hurt their economies, in an effort to pay the millions of government employees who have retired; or they will have to sharply cut pension payouts. For both government and industrial pensions, the percentage increase they pay out to supposedly compensate for inflation will continue to drop over time. Slowly but steadily, they will cease to meet the actual rate of inflation, causing the recipients' real income to drop steadily year by year. Some entities may employ one shell game or another to hide the fact that the actual buying power of pension payouts has significantly decreased, but that won't alter the reality for or the impact on the affected retirees.

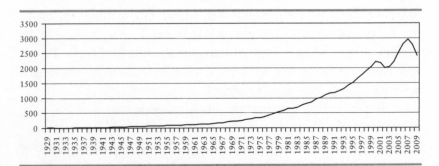

FIGURE 5.3 Current Federal Tax Receipts
Source: Bureau of Economic Analysis.

And that's not the worst of it. At least those with pensions will get something—for a while. The working poor who were never able to save will get only an increasingly paltry Social Security payment, if they qualify. More and more people will never be able to really retire; instead, they will have to take part-time jobs, working here and there for cash until the day they die. They will be forced to focus on survival. If they are lucky, they may end up living with a family that cares. Many who do not have that option will face the very real threat of sharing crowded apartments, or living on the street or in shelters of one kind or another.

More than any other group, the demise of our economy has devastated what used to be the middle class. Most in this demographic watched as their ability to get a pension was eliminated with the rise of individual retirement accounts (IRAs). IRAs are great in good times, but terrible in bad times. Instead of retiring as millionaires, as many expected, or at least nominally comfortable, many find that what little value remains in their IRAs is no match against inflation. The lucky or smart ones kept the old house; they resisted the temptation to upgrade beyond their means, only to lose a home that was too big. The more debt they took on near retirement, the more likely these former middle-class folks are to become part of the new poor. These new poor then lose the luxury to choose to retire; they must keep going until poor health forces them out of the workforce. They live with the extreme modesty of those who realize they are lucky to have a roof over their heads, and learn to be satisfied with less. Those in the middle class who circled the wagons early enough, and likely never went down the consumer debt rat hole, probably still own the home they raised their kids in, and count themselves among the fortunate. They do not talk of second homes in Florida or Arizona; they manage to get by, and hope their community is safe from crime and blight.

The rich, in contrast, are a funny sort when they face economic decay. The superrich are always going to be okay; they, in fact, thrive, no matter what happens. Bill Gates and his ilk have contingencies against almost everything; they are hardly touched even in times of war or pestilence, rather like the Rothschild banking family managed to survive in occupied Europe during World War II, in spite of being Jewish.

Below the superrich are the new rich and the barely rich. In my observation, these two groups often care deeply about their image, by today's standards; and in spite of maybe owning a business or land, or having a lot of money in stocks, also carry a lot of debt. Their wealth is mostly a façade, supported by money borrowed to pay for the house and complete remodeling, to buy high-end luxury cars, afford private schools for their kids, and other external marks of success. These two groups are very often cash-poor, if they have assets left at all. Such people are at extreme financial risk during economic decay. Debt does not go away just because that expensive house is worth so much less today; stocks drop in value, and businesses are very hard to sell during downturns. Those who have overreached will be very lucky to be holding out in the middle class in the dire future we face, unless we take proactive steps now to change things. Money is either a good servant or terrible master, depending on folks' spending habits. The new rich who had very high incomes but did not bother to build up serious money in truly safe forms will rapidly drop out of this ranking; they might even lose it all and become part of the new poor. The irony will not be lost on them, and the squeal they will make when they go to Washington looking for a bailout will be very loud. But Washington won't have the resources to do anything for them, even if legislators were so inclined.

Yes, the superrich do manage to get richer, and the poor do get poorer; but that isn't the worst of it. It isn't only the poor who are likely to get poorer, but also the middle class and the less rich or new rich. As the middle class shrinks to a fraction of its current size, the numbers of poor creep toward becoming the largest sector of American society.

It is our middle class that pays most of the bills in our society. They pay for our government—meaning the schools, police, interest on the national debt, and other costs of keeping society ticking along smoothly. Their demise as a social and economic class undermines government's ability to fund itself at the city, state, and federal levels. Already today, many cities and some states are confronting severe economic hardship; their citizens need serious help just when tax revenues are falling sharply. Every year, our federal government's debt situation looks more like that of Greece or some third-world nation. Far from being able to bail out the cities and states, the federal government will find itself in an unprecedented financial bind (Figure 5.2).

The taxes paid by the middle class will be sorely missed, when many of the services we consider basic today cease to be available. A community not far from where I live just laid off its entire police force of 26 men and women. The local government assures its citizens it can rely on the county sheriff's department to maintain law and order—as if the sheriff has any extra budget or police officers on hand to fill the gap. What will it be like in 10 or 20 years if things keep sinking? The rich are already hiring private security to patrol their neighborhoods, but will those who used to be in the middle class have anything left to foot the bill for such extras? Similarly with schools: With the tax base in decline, classroom sizes will just keep getting bigger, as the quality of education drops. Here, too, the rich will be able to afford to send their kids to private schools, so they will be unaffected, but the former middle class will not have that option. School districts will not be able to cover pension obligations, much less do what is right for the kids. A marked decline in our school systems would be yet another blow to the USA's ability to compete globally.

The industrialization of our nation was the single biggest factor in the rise of our middle class. It is that group that made this nation a place where the Bill Gates' of this country could thrive; not the other way around. Our deindustrialization to this point has already put the middle class under siege—the same middle class that plays such a key role in building and maintaining our society. If we sit back and do nothing, the inevitable economic judgment day will decimate the middle class, leaving us a much poorer nation, both financially and socially.

The path in the center where our economy limps along between these economic extremes is disappearing, along with our industrial base. It used to be that during recessions factories would cut shifts, and then ramp back up in the good times. In the past, this allowed rapid recovery from lesser recessions. Now those factories are not just cutting back, they're closing permanently and moving to China. Communities are being left without the local economic backbone that not only paid for those employees, but also supported dozens of local suppliers and generated local tax revenue.

The actual moment that defines a long process of decline would most likely be Washington doing what it does worst: trying to spend trillions more to fight structural issues, which can't be bought anyway. A state like California, Illinois, or New York will have become insolvent, only to turn up in Washington, hat in hand. The president and Congress will announce another emergency, and raise the government debt limits; but the Treasury will not be able to immediately borrow enough money. The Treasury could raise the interest rates the government pays, in an effort to attract investors and generate some cash. But let's assume that it is still not enough. Now, investors grow nervous, and world stock markets start moving downward. The president then calls on some apprehensive allies and twists some arms, which raises a bit more money, but it is still not nearly enough. Suddenly, funding even the day-to-day government operations looks exceedingly difficult; forget about bailing out the states. Emergency secret meetings ensue, followed by the president announcing some ridiculous lie like, "Gold has gone the way of the dinosaur," and selling the gold in Fort Knox or other assets to mysterious international investors at below market rate. This seems like sufficient response for the moment; and Wall Street stock prices even rally, briefly. It doesn't last, though, and the stock market soon responds to the more deep-seated fear and drops sharply lower. This is more bad news for our government, as tax revenue had been dependent on taxing paper profits from stock trading ever since legislators allowed our industrial base to be moved abroad.

The realization that tax revenue will be in steep decline finally causes the understanding to sink in that government truly is unable to fund its own needs. This feeds panic; interest rates soar while the dollar sinks and sinks in value against other currencies. The president announces yet another emergency. The states begging for aid get turned away; and sharp cuts in government employment, spending, and, eventually, pension payments are the only alternative future, beyond the nuclear solution of defaulting on our debt. If the federal government stops making interest payments on the debt, the house of cards it built will collapse. Game over. At that point no one will voluntarily loan our government any more money for many, many years.

Just when the need is higher, we are already seeing large cuts in some areas of government employment. The United States Postal Service (USPS) shrunk by tens of thousands of people in 2009. Local and state governments have let go tens of thousands. Revenue is way off in the wake of falling home prices, lower spending cutting sales tax revenue, and lower income cutting income tax revenue.[2] The economic downturn is hurting nearly every community, but the many also hit by our deindustrialization are fielding multiple blows at once—layoffs, falling wages, rising pension costs, and a sharp drop in local tax revenue—at the same time their local populations need them most.

Churches and charities will help to some degree, but even those that usually can weather most economic downturns will be forced to stretch their resources thinner and thinner. Often, people become more generous in their giving early in a recession, but the deeper and longer the downturn, the less able they are to respond to the ever more urgent requests for assistance. Within a year or two, giving to charities would drop sharply, just when demand for their assistance was surging.

Many city governments and local charities do not have a large reserve of money saved beyond what is required for the mildest of recessions. The deeper and more extended the downturn, the more strained their fiscal resources. City governments will cut back on services and, eventually, pensions to those who are about to or have already retired. The next step is much more radical: They will join cities like Maywood, California, in bankruptcy. Many charities will simply cease to exist. Those big enough to have borrowed from banks will have to address the same issue so many businesses are now dealing with: lack of cash sufficient cash flow, which leads to bankruptcy.

The deindustrialization of our nation makes both personal and business bankruptcy a lot more common, which in turn sends further shock waves through our economy. Bankruptcy is all about cash flow. Cash flow is the stream of money into businesses or other entities over time. Money comes in and goes out, depending on whether an entity is spending or earning cash. A farmer spends his or her savings, or borrows money, to buy seed to plant in the spring, hoping to collect that cash back, plus more, when he or she sells the harvested crop in the fall. During the Great Depression, many farmers were not able to earn enough cash when they sold their crops to pay back loans for the seed. Those who did not have additional cash, and could not borrow more or raise it in some other way, defaulted on their loans and lost their farms. Contrary to public opinion, it is not profit or loss that forces a company, person, charity, or local government into bankruptcy. Actual bankruptcy is almost always caused by default on a loan, debt to a supplier, or money owed to employees that the business cannot pay.

One of the many part-time jobs I held in high school and college was in a restaurant that turned out to have cash flow issues. To my surprise, one day its bank would not cash my paycheck. The restaurant got the bank to extend it more credit that week; but soon after, it closed. Looking back I can see that the proprietors had spent too much, even on cars and such, in good times and thus could not respond appropriately in downtimes.

Some businesses survive many years of losing money on paper, and yet remain solvent because they have positive cash flow or sufficient cash reserves or credit to get through the bad times. Other businesses appear to be profitable on paper, but eventually face bankruptcy because they do not have enough cash to avoid default when confronted with a challenge. This has been notable with real estate developers in recent years, which seemed very profitable and had a lot of assets, thanks to the value of land; but when the economy turned down, they had insufficient cash to make loan payments.

Just like businesses, people, charities, and governments can have cash flow problems that lead to default and bankruptcy. Even some people with excellent jobs and high salaries borrowed too much money for houses and cars, and ran up credit card debt, and thus were at risk of default and bankruptcy when the economy started to turn down. Their defaults hurt others who were owed money or had been doing business with them, and many of those others in turn cut jobs and other spending. As the economy continues to decay, more and more people default, even if they basically did everything right. A woman who loses her job and remains unemployed for a year or two, and cannot sell her home for what she paid, may be in danger of default and bankruptcy even if she never used a credit card in her life. In general, the less debt and more savings a person has, the less likely it is that short-term issues will drive him or her into default. The more a person—or for that matter, a company, charity, or government— lives beyond his or her means, the more likely it is that he or she will be at risk early of cash flow problems, even during good economic times. Some people by their nature are hard to help, but if a structural issue like deindustrialization is causing default and bankruptcy to

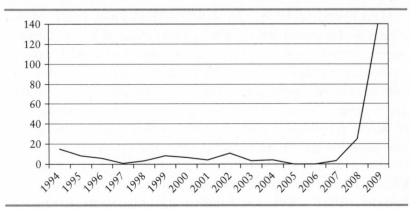

FIGURE 5.4   U.S. Bank Failures
Source: FDIC.gov.

spread rampantly, millions will be hurt in the chain reaction. Those who get caught in such a financial squeeze just before retirement might never fully recover financially (see Figure 5.4).

A large number of banks have closed in recent years. As traditional business customers like local factories faded, local and even larger banks turned to real estate developers and contractors during the housing bubble. Our shrinking manufacturing base makes it harder for these banks to diversify, and many paid the price when the housing bubble burst.

Banks are unique in that they have financial problems of their own—at the same time, they are also a big part of the economic problems we are all facing. Though the government talks about getting the banks to loan more money to small business, they are also compelling the banks to hold more money in reserve; the reality, then, is a lot fewer loans. Of course, the banks were all too willing to get more conservative in their lending *after* the damage was done. With hundreds of banks going under due to the collapsed housing market, the banks that have survived so far have cut way back on loans to small and middle-sized businesses. Businesses that depended on banks to provide loans for inventory, investment, or even to make payroll in tough times are finding it very difficult to get credit with these now-tightfisted banks. Understandably, banks do not want to make any further bad bets; but the worse the situation gets, the more lack of liquidity chokes off business activity, leading to even more economic decay.

Many companies borrow seasonally to stock up on items before a certain buying period. Retailers must spend ahead of time to be ready for the winter holiday season. The average retailer hits the breakeven point for the year only in late November. Credit has become very tight because of the many issues the banks are dealing with, so they are loaning a lot less money to businesses that desperately need resources to build or buy for their busy season. That means not just that these businesses are reducing their inventories going into the busy season, but also that they are forced to lay off employees. The chain effect of economic damage grows longer: Suppliers to these businesses chart lower sales figures and, consequently, have to lay off their employees. The former employees of both the businesses and their suppliers face extended unemployment. Until credit becomes available for businesses, the economy will not recover.

Small and midsize businesses create 70 percent of new jobs in our country; however, they are also especially vulnerable to economic downturns due to insufficient cash reserves. Fluctuations in cash flow can hurt any company, but big corporations usually have money in the bank, or credit lines, to help them pay their employees even if a big customer does not pay for some reason. Many small businesses live hand to mouth, with cash received today going toward paying their employees tomorrow. Many entrepreneurs take only a small salary or none at all. Moreover, they and their families are often the main source of investment capital in the business. Even in good times, owners of small business often have to cosign for business loans, putting them on the hook even if the business fails. Many small businesses were even started using the owner's credit card. In these cases, that person, and in effect his or her own money, is the first line of defense in dealing with cash flow issues, including not taking a salary if there is not enough cash in a given month. A bad few months, particularly now that the banks are so conservative, can wipe out the weakest small businesses. That said, there is only so long even the more stable small businesses can survive under these circumstances. A key component to our economic growth is also the most vulnerable. Economic judgment day would wipe out the majority of them, taking away with them that vital job growth.

Consumers, folks like you and me, come up against similar sorts of cash flow issues. Revenue is income from our jobs, any interest from money in a bank, dividend income, or any other source of income. Expenses are what we spend every month. Fixed expenses are those that typically do not change, like a house payment or rent. We are all vulnerable to economic downturns, but as the economy collapses, tens of millions of us who would ordinarily be okay will melt down financially. Those whose income is based on commissions will find they are taking huge pay cuts. And, of course, anyone in deep debt will be most vulnerable. As the economy continues to decline, even folks who did everything right will be filing for bankruptcy, in the tens of millions.

Bankruptcy for individuals is typically portrayed by bankruptcy lawyers on radio and television ads as an easy solution, when in fact it decimates a family's savings and often hurts their credit rating and ability to make up for lost ground before retirement. This is especially true for those close to retirement. The more we can grow the economy through buying what we make, the more we can help millions keep their good jobs and avoid bankruptcy.

If we go blindly down the path of decline, we will most likely remember economic judgment day as the day the foreigners stopped buying our debt, pulled their money out of the United States, and the dollar value collapses. Something that in reality took many years to decay will seem to collapse overnight. The usual contrived urgency expressed by legislators would suddenly take on a very hysterical pitch. Declines in the stock market and problems at major banks would have leaders of those industries back in Washington. However, anyone with any common sense will see the jig is up when Washington cannot even cover day-to-day expenses like payroll. The shock of a superpower going into a default situation, like Greece, but without Germany and the rest of the EU to bail it out would severely hurt world markets, as everyone tries to sell investments.

Given the alarming increase in the national debt, the default on a national level would be a possible, even likely, scary scenario (see Figure 5.5). Government officials would try to couch it in pretty words at first, but any move to extend debt terms because the federal government is unable to pay is, in actuality, a default. That would rapidly become glaringly obvious to the world and any country that might have considered buying our debt. At that point, the weakest cities and several states would probably have already defaulted, too;

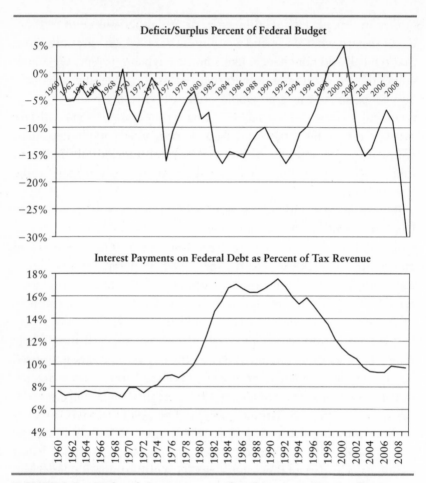

FIGURE 5.5   Federal Government Tax Revenue, Expenditures, and Borrowing

but the shock of the federal government confronting these issues would throw several dozen other deficit-prone states and many more cities into liquidity crises, as well.

Governments usually try to be part of the solution during economic downturns, but if we reach meltdown, ours will be a serious part of the problem. Even if legislators barely manage to avoid default, the huge budget deficit—which, by the way, excludes underfunded government pensions of hundreds of billions—will inhibit their ability take positive action when we need it. Just as the USPS is already radically shrinking staff, government at every level will shed employees by the hundreds of thousands, at the worst possible moment for the economy. Instead of bringing home a safe paycheck, all those families affected will become a further strain on an already weakened unemployment insurance system. Far from helping to fix things, our government will become a bigger and heavier drag on our economy.

Remember that, in the end, it was not an invasion of the homeland that took down the Spanish Empire; it was financial collapse. Even after taking vast wealth from the New World, or perhaps partially because of it, Spain gave away its capability to produce locally, and ended up borrowing from foreigners to sustain its level of consumption. Once the country defaulted and faced financial ruin, it lost its superpower status and went into an advanced state of decay. There are many similarities between our current situation and the one just described, except it took Spain much longer to mess things up. If we do not make a conscious decision to take the road to renewal, our military capabilities will decay rapidly, as well. We will not be able to buy sufficient materials, or transport them to where we need them. Training for new soldiers will be cut to below standard, or even safe, levels—actually, this appears to already be an issue. The government will commit us to military efforts abroad that we are unable to follow through on. Care for injured soldiers later in life would be compromised; and if the government is in a default scenario, even pensions for those soldiers who have put in their 20 years will be in danger of reduction. The real cost will be in the lives of our soldiers at the front, wherever that may be, and the decline in world freedom and democracy, which will naturally follow our reduced ability to nurture and protect it. At some point, we could easily end up with our troops in some foreign nation where the politicians have sent them, but without the resources to ensure they succeed. Lives are at stake. Defeat *is* possible.

We are looking at two very real alternatives in regard to unemployment. In the good scenario, we move toward full employment, with an unemployment rate of 3 to 4 percent. That situation allows for students to find relevant jobs upon graduation; it also makes it possible to welcome back anyone, like mothers, who want to reenter the workforce. The negative alternative features high unemployment, including those who have given up, in the 20 percent or more range (see Figure 5.6). Try as it might, the government will not be able to

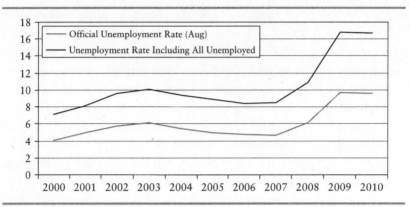

FIGURE 5.6   Standard Unemployment Rate versus Total Rate (Aug)

solve the problem of extended high unemployment rates without resorting to tricks, like boosting housing construction artificially.

Perpetual double-digit unemployment is entirely possible if we do not take decisive action to protect and nurture our industrial base. The long-term social effect will be an entire generation that has a near-complete lack of opportunity to find a job that makes a real contribution, much less follow their dreams (see Figure 5.7). Previous generations of Americans never questioned their stake in our culture and society, but today, as during the Great Depression, future

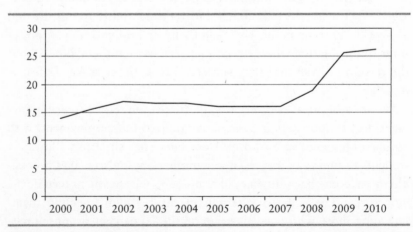

FIGURE 5.7   Unemployment Rate Among Those 16 to 20 (Aug)

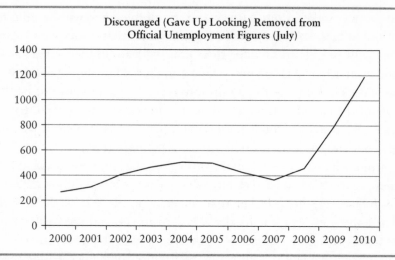

FIGURE 5.8   Labor Force Statistics from the Current Population Survey

generations have no real hope of finding a decent job (see Figure 5.8) and, therefore, little chance to enjoy the benefits of our society, such as buying a home. Life is cheap for those who do not feel they are a part of something greater in our country. Those of us who have good jobs that add value have a great deal to lose should there be a breakdown in the positive social order. In effect, we own a share in our country and its future. It is not always the case, but those who have no share in our country's future act much more like renters than owners. Owners typically take much better care of property than renters. We will see this on a massive scale if our nation makes it impossible for entire future generations to claim ownership in our society. Americans used to be the sort who automatically lent a hand to a neighbor in need. Higher and extended unemployment would change the very core of our society. Poverty would increase, the standard of living would drop, and America would become a harsher and more dangerous place to live, a place where people look out only for themselves, where crime surges and is less likely to be punished, and where fear outweighs hope.

An America remade, a country that fosters its industry, will defeat high unemployment—the first of our true enemies—and with that, generations of Americans will get jobs in which they can add real value that all can appreciate. In doing so, they will be able to claim an important stake in our society and its future: They will be able to afford homes, and enjoy the financial security that comes with them; they will be able to save for their kids' education, their retirement, and even a fun vacation every now and then. Hardship and sacrifice should have a chance to pay off into something valuable, not be the rule of the day. The fractures that are already spreading throughout our culture can be stopped; moreover, they can be healed, if we just give our citizens an opportunity to do something great.

Ironically, the power to make this change has been in our hands all these years. We just need to buy what we make so that those trillions of dollars stay here, rather than subsidizing the rest of the world. The longer we wait, the harder it will be to act, and the weaker our economy will grow. To act now, before our wealth and resources are completely depleted, is difficult, to be sure, but much easier than waiting until after our collapse. Acting in the near term means we dictate the terms and have control of the situation. Waiting means the terms will be dictated to us by foreign creditors.

TWO

How America's Competitors Are Taking Advantage of Us

Chapter 6 China's Grand Game

The Rise of a Superpower

China is already becoming the world's "other" superpower, economically and politically. It aims to be the next number one superpower, ending the United States' brief time on top, by design and default. How did it gain this economic and political might so rapidly, sailing past the Russians and Europeans and edging quickly up on the United States? How was China able to grasp the golden ring when so many other nations were unable to do so? How was it possible for the Chinese to pick up the ball that we have dropped?

Their effort was intentional, and has been well planned. History provides penetrating insight into their motivation. No civilization still in existence has a longer history than China. A landmass of roughly the same size as the United States, China has seen regular cycles of cities and provinces coming together or breaking up. The country has always been heavily populated relative to other nations; today, the majority of its 1.2 billion people live in the coastal provinces on the east side of the nation. The population density, particularly in these coastal provinces, has always been high. Some areas are quite good for farming, and with optimal rainfall produce surplus crops, which contributed to the population growth. Over time, having sufficient food and more than enough people to do the farming freed others to develop more diverse skills, such as in construction and the arts, which led to the emergence of early civilizations. The Chinese were developing writing and other advanced traits of society while my forefathers were still wearing animal skins.

However, this dense population also left the country crowded, relative to the rest of the world, and therefore more susceptible to suffering caused by disease or starvation, in the event of drought, flood, or other natural disaster. Civilization brings many benefits, but it also seems to encourage the development of weapons and social organizations that can multiply the intensity and rapidity of destruction. Human-induced tragedy, like war and oppression, has been very common in China throughout its history. The country is more culturally and racially diverse than many Americans realize, with 23 different minority groups. The population is dominated by the Han ethnic group, at 92 percent.[1] Over China's long history, the Han have typically controlled politics, except during periods when barbarians from the north have seized power. Even the barbarians usually ended up ruling through local Han officials, however, as they eventually became civilized by the very people they had conquered.

In Chinese, the country name means "Center Nation," reflecting the historic belief that the country is the center of the world. The nation's capitol, Beijing (meaning "Northern Capital") is not at the center of the nation, but very far north, near the Great Wall. Beijing is much closer to China's traditional enemies, the barbaric horsemen known as the Mongols, and their cousins, so it makes sense that the ruling capital would develop where they could most effectively respond to the strongest outside threat. The north historically being the dangerous enemy frontier brought about the construction of the Great Wall, in stages, between 7 and 3 BC.[2] The construction site also served as a giant prison camp, where the emperor of the day disposed of many thousands of potential enemies. Though 4,500 miles long, the wall did not turn out to be the effective defense hoped for, since some gatekeepers proved willing to take bribes.

On the western frontier, along the traditional Silk Road, lies the land of Tibet, now considered a Chinese province by the government. Nepal and India are beyond that. Mountainous territory and extreme desert conditions have prevented the people of the west from becoming much of a concern. In the south dwell another of China's traditional enemies, the Vietnamese; but China has been more likely to cause them trouble, so they were never considered a threat. Also in the south are Thailand, Cambodia, Laos, and Myanmar (formerly Burma).

The last true ethnically Chinese empire, the Ming, was removed from power by the Manchu, more horse-riding barbarians from the north, who founded the Qing Dynasty in 1644.[3] This did not happen overnight, but over the next several decades, with the Manchu seizing the north in a series of successful raids and invasions, and then pushing south to further exert their control. Once the main capital of the day's kingdom or empire fell to an invader, revolution, or rival, the provinces split off into smaller kingdoms. Those new kingdoms naturally had their own views about who should be on top. These cycles of order, decline, chaos, and reunification have continued for millennia in China. Before Rome, before Greece, at approximately the same time that the oldest Indian or Egyptian cultures were forming along the Nile River, China's history was already germinating.

The Qing Dynasty was already in an advanced state of decline when a new enemy appeared from the sea, the Europeans. This was the age when the British, French, Spanish, and even the Portuguese (Macao) were rapidly building empires of their own around the globe. They came to China for spices, gold, trade, and, later, territory; but at this point, tea became a big market in Europe, particularly for the British. At the time, China was the only source of tea. The Chinese, however, did not want much the British had to offer. The British did have one thing that was in great demand in China—opium. So when the British ran out of silver, they were quick to move to profit from the demand for the drug. Naturally, the Chinese government resisted, in spite of its weakened condition. This sparked the first Opium War, ending in the British seizure of the territory that later became Hong Kong, along with an advantageous trade agreement.

This in turn led to a serious of altercations and more territory seizures by the British and other European powers. The Bundt section of Shanghai is a very obvious reminder that it was once German territory, and not so very long ago in historical terms. Meanwhile, the Manchu power was splintering. Warlords and revolutionaries rose in this vacuum to struggle for power, among them Mao Zedong's Communists and Chiang Kai-shek's Nationalists.

The Nationalists were favored by the West; Communists by the young Soviet Union. Initially, they worked together, nominally, as the Qing collapsed. Then the Nationalists turned on the Communists, in a secret plot to exterminate them, but were unable to succeed sufficiently to stop the movement. Among the individuals who escaped was Mao, and he led the remnants of the Communists on the famous "long march," to escape.

In spite of their connections to warlords and Chinese mafia ("triads"), the Americans heavily supported the Nationalists, in the form of money, weapons, and resources. The motivation may have been simply that there was no obvious choice with cleaner hands that actually had a chance to rule in the immediate term. I have spent time in many countries, and read a great deal of history, yet know of no occasion when the USA has won a struggle by reaching out to a local generalissimo with bloody hands.

There are, however, many instances when we have successfully supported peoples who were already reaching for liberty and democracy, such as most of Eastern Europe. Sticking to our principles and strategically seeding democracy and freedom, with our eyes on the future, instead of focusing on short-term body counts, completely shifts the dynamic for generations to come. It is a lot more pleasant and effective in the long run for the USA to reach our goals when the young people protesting are standing for democracy, and not against some petty tyrants on our payroll.

While America was supporting the Nationalists, Japan was grabbing China's northern territory, founding Manchukuo in 1932, and invading the rest of China in 1937.[4] The vicious fighting left huge numbers of civilian casualties, and Japan in control of the entire coastal region and beyond. The Nationalists and recovering Communists again threw in together, but American aid was only able to reach them either through Burma in the far south or over the Himalaya mountains via British-controlled India. Neither of these routes was at all efficient, so aid only trickled in. But the Japanese were having problems of their own. The naval war in the Pacific, which had gone so well for the Japanese early in the conflict, had drastically overextended their resources. The USA's victory at Midway Island (where, as I mentioned in Chapter 1, we lost the aircraft carrier Yorktown, and the Japanese Imperial Navy lost three key aircraft carriers in one day) had turned the tide. Meanwhile, in mainland China, the Chinese were unable to repel the Japanese; in turn, the Japanese were unable to extinguish the Chinese resistance. To this day, more than 65 years later, the treatment of civilians by the Japanese army is remembered vividly in China for its harsh brutality.

Japan's surrender to the United States left a surreal power gap in China. In theory, the Japanese were only supposed to surrender to the Nationalists, meaning the Japanese were to turn over their weapons and equipment to them. Through corruption and incompetence, the Nationalists never managed to gain the trust of the people. For example, there is no evidence of the party reaching out to the agrarian masses that made up the lion's share of the population in that day. Even with the material advantages handed to them at the end of the World War II, and significant continued support from the United States, the situation returned to open civil war. Far from winning, the Nationalists found themselves on the defensive, and losing ground all over the nation. In 1949, they threw in the towel and left for the island of Formosa, just off the Chinese coast, which would be renamed Taiwan.[5] They remain there to this day. This loss was historically the biggest in the U.S. effort to support supposed democracy around the world, albeit through another corrupt junta. This was far from the last time our strategy of backing such factions would backfire.

The Communists ruthlessly consolidated power by killing millions, initially with the help of the Soviet Union. Before long, though, the Russian and Chinese Communists turned on each other. Supposed international Communism could not get past historic national rivalries. China had almost no industry to speak of, no strong central government for more than 50 years, and had suffered massive civil war, invasion, and more civil war. Such was the environment that forged the views of its leadership.

The Communists consolidated power and started to rebuild their economy, and soon thereafter started meddling in other nations' affairs, including Vietnam and Cambodia and others in Africa and South America. We fought them briefly during the Korean War. After our daringly executed naval invasion at Inchon left the North Koreans reeling, in 1950, Chinese forces crossed the border using human-wave strategies to overwhelm Allied positions, in spite of suffering horrific casualties.

China developed nuclear weapons in 1964,[6] and became a member of the United Security Council in 1971.[7]

Pragmatists and politicians on both sides—most notably, Mao, Richard Nixon, and Henry Kissinger—reopened relations between China and the United States with Nixon's trip to China in 1972, a first for an American president.[8] A friend in Asian public service during that era told me that during their meeting in Beijing, Mao himself fed food into Nixon's mouth, in an attempt to curry his favor. Although my friend wasn't present at that meeting, his former position and the atmosphere surrounding U.S.–Chinese relations at that time make the story plausible.

With such a lengthy history, especially one involving the rise and fall of so many civilizations over the millennia, it is little wonder that Beijing takes a longer-term view than our leadership. By absorbing our manufacturing capability, we think that we can save some money on that shirt, pair of shoes, or other item today; in contrast, they think in terms of the world they could own and control tomorrow.

Could it have been Nixon landing in Beijing in the ultramodern Air Force One that planted the seeds in the minds of Mao and his cohorts that grew into the decision to grasp superpower status through modernization?

It is difficult to describe, but hundreds of years of overpopulation have evolved into a culture whose members have a very different view of sacrifice and life and death than ours in the West. Maybe it is harder to relate to an individual's suffering when there are so many in distress. Perhaps people become hardened to life and death when they have seen so much misery. It is an ugly way to describe it, but life is just held cheaper in much of Asia, though I have seen that changing with modernization in places like Japan, Singapore, and Korea.

In the USA, if a child falls down a well, it is national news. In China, it would likely not even make the local papers. Who is to say which is better or more appropriate? In my mind, our Western view that life is precious is superior; but we do need to understand that the context in which other major powers see things is different.

If Winston Churchill or Franklin Roosevelt would have said, "We will pay any price," the meaning of that statement would have been very different from what dictators like Joseph Stalin or Mao meant. In the West it means that we work hard every day, and the leader pins a medal on those who accomplish what we set out to achieve. Whereas for leaders like Stalin or Mao, history has shown that such a statement is a personal promise that their own people will pay any price. Even if a million are ground into dust, a hundred million more are ready to take their place, followed by a million more who were born just last month.

China had one overwhelming resource available even after the chaos of World War II and civil war—people. Overpopulation is self-perpetuating: Too many people produce too many people, and then some. During and shortly after consolidation of power, the Communists encouraged higher birthrates. Eventually, they realized they were being overwhelmed and instituted a one-child-per-family strategy, with very serious repercussions for those who did not obey. They still had far too many people, but succeeded in controlling growth—if ruthlessly.

Industry implies making items with machines, instead of people doing it by hand, so initially it must have been with some trepidation that China, an overpopulated nation, embraced industrialization. On the other hand, it must have been clear that even a million people working with their hands could not build Air Force One. Only modernization could lead to such advanced machines.

With a huge army, ever-present state police, and nuclear weapons, the Chinese leaders could, for the foreseeable future, feel secure in their own power to block future invasions or prevent humiliations like those they had experienced so often in the last 50 years. However, without modern factories they could not have much influence over anyone beyond their own immediate neighbors. The European and Japanese invasions of China, in particular, showed what a relatively small number of troops could do with modern weapons. The human-wave strategy used in the Korean War had proven its point to the United States about China's regard for human life, but also must have demonstrated how quickly the machines, like aircraft, could attack and defeat the massing soldiers.

China's leaders had consolidated power, but other small nations were becoming more modern, and therefore more powerful as well. Only industrialization would give China the capacity to truly be able to shake off history and become a world power. *The* world power.

If this was not obvious to Mao himself, it was clear to a young and rising power in the party, Deng Xiaoping. Various party loyalists held power after Mao's death, but when Xiaoping succeeded to power in 1978, things went into overdrive. He even grasped certain ideals of capitalism and created free trade zones. What initially seemed to me, young and green and believing so fervently in Adam Smith, a vindication of capitalism actually became gateways through which China could import technology and build industrial and political strength. Hundreds of factories were set up to take advantage of cheap labor, and these were used as models for many thousands more to be built in later years throughout China.

The Chinese must have been amazed by how quickly the West and its Asian allies lined up to sell them technology they would otherwise have needed years or decades to develop themselves. Our shortsighted view of immediate economic return, versus the long-term cost, again got in our way. Our business leaders' greed and Washington's naïveté came up against a complex nation that is truly willing to pay any price for eventual dominance.

What if China and these other nations had said to us 20 or 30 years ago that we must close our factories and put tens of millions of our citizens out of work? That we would be required to take cheaper, lower-quality goods from them for now, nudging us toward the edge of the economic abyss? That they would take our money and loan back some to allow Washington to—briefly—sustain its spending addiction, but in just a few years would dominate us economically? Had the terms been explicit, had we seen the ultimate outcome of the alliances we formed and deals we made, we would have been appalled. I like to think that we would have blocked the way immediately, cutting off the road to our own decline. But no one laid out the plan for us, and our leadership didn't see it. Slowly, from our in-the-moment point of view, but quickly from their historical point of view, we have been eased with comforting words toward the door to historical obscurity. Surely, if they had been open about their real intent, if they were open even now, we would stand up and take notice. We would move back toward a self-sustaining economy.

It hasn't been in the open, it hasn't been laid out for us, and this is what has happened: Our businesses have opened the door and invited China in, and in doing so have handed that country the means to orchestrate our downfall and step into America's place in the world. The Chinese could hardly have imagined more cooperative allies in this effort than our own soulless retail corporations, which I know from firsthand observation are led by executives concerned for little beyond this quarter's profit and their own bonuses.

Ironically, we have handed over the keys to China via our own corporations. Our large retail chains have led the way in opening our markets so rapidly to these imported products, causing so much stress on our capability to produce products here. Wal-Mart, as I said, is the single biggest importer of goods from China. The company's determined effort to focus only on price has forced all the other chains to take similar actions. More than any other major nation, we leave national companies free to act in their own interests. But we should take notice, and action, when they—wittingly or unwittingly—assist in undermining our national interest. (I'll discuss this in more depth in Chapter 8.)

The business media I read daily often presents a view of the world through American eyes, as if all world companies, individuals, and governments have the same sort of motivations. This is especially true with regard to trade, where business pundits righteously talk about "free trade" as if it is a basic human right. My direct observation from living in Asia for a total of seven years is that there is no such thing as free trade. It is only free coming here to the USA. Exports to other nations from here are vastly more difficult, because those nations look out for their own interests first. This is especially the case with China, which is not playing by the free trade rules as we define them, not by a long shot. China is playing a national mercantile game, whereby the country rightly views a strong manufacturing base as key to becoming the next superpower. If the Chinese can bluff us into closing our own industrial base, and watch us weaken ourselves dramatically, all the better, from their point of view.

The ancient Chinese general and philosopher Sun Tzu wrote, "Hence to fight and conquer in all your battles is not supreme excellence; supreme excellence consists in breaking the enemy's resistance without fighting."[9] He meant that on many levels. War itself is just one method of achieving a political goal.

Sun Tzu also strongly encouraged spying on potential enemies and other indirect means to undermine them, which also costs money but is much cheaper than open warfare. Building wealth resources is necessary to a politically strong state. Depriving a potential enemy of its wealth is second nature to Chinese strategic politics today, just as it was to Sun Tzu more than 2,000 years ago.

This is not exactly political rocket science, yet where are we, the United States today, on this measure? We are running a huge trade deficit with the Chinese; indeed, they are the top foreign creditor funding Washington's spending! Not only have we walked into this trap, but, as I said earlier, we opened the door and invited them in. Because we owe them so much money—much of which originated within the USA—they are already indirectly shaping our trade and economic policies (see Figures 6.1 and 6.2). Where was the first place Hillary Clinton flew when she took over as Secretary of State? Our old allies in Europe? No. Neighbors with issues, like Mexico? No. It was Tokyo, on her way to Beijing. She had to take care of our bankers first.

China is achieving its goals more effectively than the nation's leaders could have possibly hoped, because of our own weakness.

How Much Is China Funding Our Federal Government Borrowing?

	2002	2003	2004	2005	2006	2007	2008
China Direct U.S. Debt (Treasury) Ownership (Billions of $)	118.4	159	222.9	310	396.9	477.6	727.4
Increase Year to Year		40.6	63.9	87.1	86.9	80.7	249.8
U.S. Fed Gov't Borrowing (Billions of $)		553.3	531.1	418.3	291.6	408.1	912.3
% of New USA Fed Borrowing Funded by China		7.3%	12.0%	20.8%	29.8%	19.8%	27.4%

Source: Congressional Research Service Report, "China's Holding of U.S. Securities: Implications for U.S. Economy," June 30, 2009.
Source: Bureau of Economic Analysis.
Analysis: Todd Lipscomb

FIGURE 6.1   How Much Is China Funding Our Federal Government Borrowing?

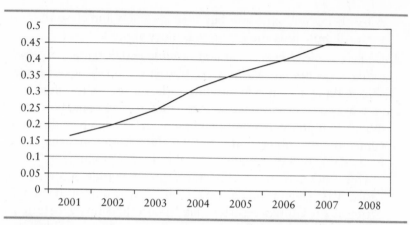

FIGURE 6.2   China's U.S. Dollar Reserves (Debt, Cash, and Securities) Holdings As a Percent of Total Chinese GDP
Source: Congressional Research Service Report, "China's Holding of U.S. Securities: Implications for U.S. Economy," June 30, 2009.

Our media may believe there is a sort of internationalist movement of brothers, but as we sink, the rest of the world is playing the same old game of nations, to determine who will lead the future.

China's key advantages stem from this history versus the United States:

1. *China today has a much longer-term view than the United States.* With such a long history, it is natural the Chinese would tend to think in terms of years or decades, whereas we think in terms of weeks or months. Two hundred years and a few decades may seem like a long time to us, but our nation is very young relative to China. We are primarily concerned with immediate satisfaction, and recently that has become even more the case.

   A healthy short-term view has its advantages, like being able to deal with problems that pop up unexpectedly, such as a natural disaster. However, when dealing with economic issues such as these, we have to think in terms of years.

   Proponents of the short-term view easily become victims of clever long-term thinkers. If the long-term thinker's real goal is to usurp our industrial power, to become the next superpower, it is perfectly natural that they would sell products to us today below our cost. We shrug and tell ourselves it must just be about our wages being too high, and buy their products and close that factory. All those jobs and livelihoods move abroad.

2. *Chinese leadership is clever and resolute in achieving their goals, unlike legislators in Washington.* It is hard to imagine our leadership making a plan that is going to last a few years, much less several decades. Washington drifts from issue to issue, borrowing more and more each month, without firm leadership or direction. China on the other hand, has resolute leadership that stays focused on goals over many years; it is doing so right now.

   This is not an issue of democracy, though that does not make it easier. Past generations of leadership in Washington have been better at providing consistent leadership than this generation's leaders, from both parties.

   This might not be such a big issue for our capital if the others abroad were like Paris or Rome, but while we become less able to hold onto our national interests, Beijing never drops this ball.

   Dictatorships may have a natural advantage in being able to focus in one direction over a period of many years, but fear of that leadership often results in such projects devolving into fiascos. In a culture where the populace is afraid to criticize its government, leadership has to be clever to accomplish an established goal over many years. Hitler's generals feared telling him the truth, because of his temper and the fact that he would have them killed if they did so. This led to major errors in troop movements near the end of the war, as he ordered troops to locations based on the assumption that some were still capable fighting forces, when they no longer were. This left gaping holes in the Nazi defense, which Hitler might have been able to adjust for had he been provided with accurate information.

3. *The Chinese willingness to sacrifice human life is far beyond our scope of understanding.* In a total of seven years of living in Asia, I learned that Western culture values life differently than Eastern culture. We in this country are unique in that we would, for example, spend millions in medical treatments to give an elderly person a few more years, or even months, of life without even presuming to judge whether he or she was helping the community, or was just going to spend those added days watching reruns on television. That kind of care would be reserved for the rich and elite in most of the world. In China, if you do not have a special reason for receiving care beyond a certain age, it is generally accepted that you do not expect more.

It is not that parents love their children less from one culture to another; it is a cultural difference in the way folks are taught to view life and death. One the first things I noticed living abroad was that the sound of children playing, and their laughter, is the same everywhere.

China's goal to be the next dominant superpower hinges on too much industrialization too quickly, taking a huge human toll in the form of on-the-job accidents and pollution exposure. There is no real worker's compensation for industrial accidents. Once, when I was in a shop in China looking at computer equipment, I noticed an attractive young woman in her midtwenties working there whose hands looked as if they had been dipped in acid. Another victim of industrialization. You see them on the streets, away from the capital and main city downtown areas: people with serious injuries, even missing limbs, suffering and struggling. For this woman at the shop, her hands were mostly still functional, enabling her to locate or buy her way into another job.

This cultural difference is hard to explain in a few sentences, even for me after all those years in Asia. It seems to stem from an idea that we will all die anyway; it is only a matter of when. Combining their view with the way we value life might inspire some to really "live life," create art, or otherwise change the way we spend our time. In my case, it led me to quit a lucrative executive job to help America, through the founding of MadeinUSAForever.com, and my efforts to raise awareness of the current threat to the USA and what we can do about it.

In China, and indeed many places in Asia, there seems to be an easier acceptance of death. Indeed, death goes largely unnoticed and unreported, except in the most extreme cases. It took dozens of schools collapsing in a Shenzhen earthquake to prompt an official review of shoddy workmanship; thousands of babies had to sicken, and many to die, before a few of the culprits responsible for intentionally putting melamine (a plastics additive that boosts the tested protein level) in dairy products were tracked down.

China does have too many people, and thousands of years of dealing with that reality affects a culture: It creates a different view of life than ours.

The Chinese government is exploiting that fact on a massive scale, in order to absorb the world's factories. If a foreigner went there and started to impose this damage to their people and the environment, the nation would resist. Yet their government, a heavy-handed police state, nurtures widespread overindustrialization, despite unprecedented human and environmental destruction, pushing its people to their limits to claim this power.

4. *China's historic view of trade and money as tools of national policy, versus our view of business and national policy as separate, gives it a distinct advantage in today's game among nations.* It is perfectly rational for a nation with a coherent, semisecret strategy of becoming the next dominant superpower to use every tool at its disposal, particularly trade and economics. Machiavelli's *The Prince* was an influence in Europe, but Sun Tzu had a much broader effect on the game of politics and power in China. Using every available means to undermine potential enemies and achieve national goals was very much a tenet of the Chinese general. To him, war was simply another arrow among many to use to achieve those goals.

China's is a cynical kind of leadership that uses every movement and statement, public and secret, to gain power over other nations. It's also a leadership system that is alive and well in much of the world, so it's naïve, and dangerous on our part to assume the world plays by our rules.

We wonder where the power we held in 1960 went: We had never lost a major war, and controlled vast resources and industry; we led the world in technology, as well as politically and economically. Flash forward to 2011; much of that power has drained from this country. Our factories are closing by the thousands, and it is laughable to think we lead the world in electronics and many other fields. China is taking this power, cleverly easing us toward future irrelevance. The Chinese do not need to fight us in a war to win this struggle for our wealth and power. We send it over to them on every shipload of products for Wal-Mart. History will not be kind to us if we do not take a stand.

Chinese history, development, and circumstances have allowed them to develop a concerted strategy to take this power from us over decades, whereas similiar strategies brought down the foreign barbarians who managed to conquer China. The Manchu and the rest were not expelled in a climactic battle, like a scene from a movie. They pushed in with the young, virile power of barbarians, but lost their strength over the years by making a thousand small sacrifices to become civilized and enjoy luxury and comfort, until, finally, their power was only a façade, at which time their leadership was a distant memory. Our power is being sapped the same way, though not without our help.

It could be that the average person in China will one day look back with both wonder and regret, seeing the growth, but also the losses and the damage caused by releasing dangerous chemicals into their environment. Will the Chinese connect rising cancer rates with the water they drink, the air they breathe, and the food they eat? By then, a new chapter of history will have begun. Dead leaders can be vilified, but not punished.

China is gambling that it can achieve its goal of world leadership through encouraging both its own rapid growth and the United States' decline. Whether or not the effort is successful is in our hands. If we choose to wake up, take a stand, and make America great again, we can assure our ascendancy.

Stand with me for the USA. Together, we can make a big difference.

Chapter 7 The Unfair Playing Field Abroad

To read the news, one would think that the only reason U.S. manufacturing is at a disadvantage is the wage difference. Not so; it is just one piece of the puzzle. Wages are higher here, yet when I oversaw finance in Asia for an American technology company, I saw other significant factors as well, which in total have a much greater impact than the wage difference. In fact, we could sustain better wages in the United States and still outproduce our Asian competitors if we had a level playing field on these other key issues.

Other notable cost advantages in many nations, and particularly China, include savings on worker safety spending, government protection from imports, savings on environmental control spending, and currency manipulation, among others. For example, imagine that a factory in the United States and one in China are both producing sets of flatware on the newest machinery, at the rate of about 100 units per hour per worker. Often, I have seen quotes for manufacturing costs in Chinese factories that were far less than half those of the U.S. products; but for our purposes here, let's assume half—$10 for the U.S. factory and $5 for the Chinese factory. Assuming the worker here is making an average hourly rate of $25, including benefits, and the Chinese worker $2, that translates to $0.25 per unit in the United States and $0.02 in China. Standing alone, it sounds like a significant difference, but consider it in context: The $0.23 per unit wage difference is actually less than 5 percent of the total $5 cost difference! Clearly, something other than wages is impacting the cost of production, and impacting it dramatically.

Naturally, true costs vary, depending on a multitude of factors for each product out there, but in general, the wage difference is much less of a problem than the media plays it up to be. These additional factors save Chinese and third-world producers a substantial amount of money, as well—often far more than wage difference.

UNSAFE WORKING CONDITIONS

If you look beyond the few model factories in China, the ones that are "shown off" to the media and personages like Steve Jobs, to the subcontractors where most products are really made, you'd see worker conditions that are truly horrific. Owners of these smaller, dirtier, more dangerous factories simply ignore paltry local government regulations, or pay bribes instead of addressing infractions.

Mattel, Levi Strauss & Co., and other large companies may think they know who is making their products in China, but often they don't. When they contracted with companies in Hong Kong or Shanghai, probably they were shown a factory or two, but not likely the ones where most of their goods are actually made. To make a profit on the aggressive bids that won these contracts, the Chinese makers subcontract out the majority of production to smaller factories, which in turn push it to yet lower levels.

On a flight to Hong Kong, I happened to be sitting next to a buyer for Lands' End, the catalog retailer. She was telling me how great the company's contract manufacturers in China were. This was an eye-opening conversation for me, as Lands' End used to be very committed to buying American-made. I asked her how they could be sure worker conditions are up to snuff at those factories, and that the

Chinese were not counterfeiting any of their products. She assured me that they were fully inspected and had found zero violations so far. When I asked how often these inspections took place, she told me once per year. By this point I could barely contain my dismay, so I asked, "Are they given notice you are coming?" "Yes, a month beforehand," she said. I then told her that doing one inspection a year and giving them any notice at all means the entire inspection process was worthless; that she, in fact, could have no idea what the actual worker conditions were, or any real clue as to what was going on at that factory. I also told her it was very likely that a big percentage of what Lands' End buys was not even made at that nice clean facility she was visiting!

Rare inspections preceded by notice to the manufacturer are a cop-out. If retailers buying the products really cared about working conditions at these plants, not to mention the many other violations unannounced audits would turn up, they would pursue the situation.

HEROES OF OUR USA EFFORT IN THEIR OWN WORDS

Western Head to Toe—Schaefer Ranchwear

We are fully committed to producing our Ranchwear and outdoor clothing here in this great nation of ours. That's why we made the investment to have our own factory. We own a 13,500-square-foot factory, with about 75 employees.

We feel strongly that the product category we're in, call it Ranchwear or western wear, originated out in the U.S. West. From our perspective, it's a style of clothing that originated with the working cowboy. We still stay true to those roots after almost 30 years in business. It's a shame that a style of clothing that is so American is predominantly being imported today. We are the last full-line "Made in USA" western wear manufacturer left in the United States. We may be the last full-line apparel manufacturer left, period.

Owning our own factory allows us much more flexibility in production, as well as quick turnaround times and product development. Outsourcing is not an option, considering required lead times, travel, prepay terms, and minimum production requirements. We can make immediate adjustments to production based on demand. There's no way this can be done when importing product. Though the majority of our sales are

(continued)

(continued)
because we make a quality product, we do have a large following of customers who demand an American-made product. Also, our international customers originally came to us because our products are American made. Western wear imported from the Pacific Rim does not sell well internationally.

We are very lucky to have the skilled labor we do. Our factory can make just about anything. Currently, we manufacture high-needle coats and vests, shirts, and jeans. The majority of our products feature multiple pockets, heavy leather trim, pattern matches, multiple zippers, and more; they are complicated garments. We also produce and maintain stock of more than 68 styles. This demands a highly skilled and dedicated American workforce.

Producing here strengthens the whole American economy, as a result. The difficult part is getting the textile industry back on its feet. So many textile mills have gone out of business over the last 20 years. These mills are gone forever, in my opinion. Can you imagine trying to set up mills again under the current antibusiness climate? It's practically impossible. In order for apparel manufacturers to come back, there has to be a supply of raw material coming from somewhere. We're in a unique situation because we have our infrastructure already set up, and have plenty of room for expansion. Other so-called manufacturers really aren't manufacturers at all. They are just promoting a brand name and importing an apparel package.

We will always make sure Ranchwear is truly American.

Worker conditions, not to mention product safety or minimum wage rules, are almost completely ignored at the subcontractor level. Many are further contracted out to the point at which piecemeal items are assembled in homes, where children could be at risk from chemicals, or even put to work. For example, let's say a toy maker wants to launch a new doll. This maker's retail customer, WYZ-Mart, wants to sell the doll for $8.95, so the wholesale price is maybe $4.50. Excluding marketing, the CEO bonus, and other overhead, the company calculates it can make the doll for $3.00 here in the USA, meeting U.S. worker safety standards, and with zero product safety concerns. From our perspective, it sounds like everything is good; but for many companies, that's not good enough. Instead, they send an employee to Hong Kong or Guang Zhou to talk to Chinese suppliers. The visiting American is impressed with the 63 minutes he or she spends in the "clean, safe-looking" Chinese plant. Even more impressive is the replica of the new doll and the price he or she is quoted: $0.99 each. The American does not understand how the Chinese manufacturer could hit that price; nevertheless, he or she demands, and gets, $0.89 each. The Chinese supplier also agrees to meet or exceed product and worker safety standards, and the American tells them sternly that he or another American will be back to check the standards at the facility once a year, but not to worry as they will schedule that visit several weeks ahead of time.

The Chinese company underbids the true cost of the project and gets the order. It loses money at first, but the good news is that it can present itself as an international company, which helps it get credit from the bank, and maybe even eventually sell its stock on the Chinese stock market. The bad news is that it signed an order at a price that makes it impossible to profit without seriously cutting corners. Making sure a special batch is produced at the highest standards for safety testing, the company starts to search for ways to cut costs. That is not hard to do, as there are hundreds, even many thousands, of small companies in China that want a chance to work with a bigger one. So the original Chinese maker subcontracts out the majority of the production to a smaller company. That way, it can avoid cost issues like safety and minimum wage while keeping its hands relatively clean. The subcontractor likewise has some challenges to make its costs, but is not worried, as it can do what it needs to with little expectation of government interference. In fact, a local government official may be a part owner and/or on the subcontractor's board of directors. Thus, the subcontractor not only can count on lax enforcement, but even arrange police support if its workers "get ideas." Even so, the subcontractor finds profitability tough to achieve and so looks to subcontract out further. Past the point at which any semblance of quality standards are met, piecemeal work is contracted out at rates like $1.00 per thousand units assembled. This work moves into dirt-floor hovels, even homes. Who is doing that work now? This is the point at which children are exposed to chemicals, and could end up working.

This sort of chain of events is repeated many times every day. Ultra-low retail chain pricing translates into suffering, risk, and pollution somewhere else. The irony is that often those goods are as chintzy as they are cheap, and quickly get thrown away.

GOVERNMENT PROTECTION FROM IMPORTS

China, Japan, and Korea protect their own manufacturers at the expense of foreign manufacturers. The item could be declared strategic; local content rules or tariffs might be applied, safety barriers that are really just protection from imports; or a dozen other formal or informal ways might be taken to safeguard their own.

I have observed again and again how masterful they are at dodging imports, in spite of trade agreements that opened our doors to them. For example, Japan blocked the import of American apples for several decades using excuse after excuse, finally telling a story about a microbe on the apples that could hurt their trees if they were allowed into the country. Of course, the organism they were referring to was present worldwide, including on their own apples. Those Japanese experts who pointed out the scientific facts were vilified in the media as if they had betrayed their nation by pointing out a simple fact. Without realizing the government was using the microbe as an excuse to block imports, the experts pointed out the facts and undermined the government position. It was about protecting their production.

Formal and informal means used by these countries to impede the success of foreign companies are so common they reach every corner of the import process. The only companies that can break through these barriers, and it often takes many years, are well-known worldwide brands like Coca-Cola. The other exceptions, of course, are those products that they do not have in sufficient quantity, such as raw materials including metals, grain, and beef.

Not everyone in these countries feels strongly about the issue, but everyone in Japan is taught to buy Japanese first, in Korea to buy Korean first, and in China to buy Chinese first. This ingrained bias is an effective cultural barrier that is very difficult to get through; it becomes second nature. Most people there are not about to change.

We need a lot more of this thinking in the United States.

IGNORING INTELLECTUAL PROPERTY RIGHTS

In nations like China, it is common to all but ignore patents. While living in Asia, I personally witnessed multiple lawsuits underway in

China. The courts there are highly unlikely to side with foreign firms seeking to stop a Chinese firm from copying their patents, processes, methods, copyrights, or trademarks, or to enforce other intellectual property rights. Even winning such a case often results in an award of just a few thousand dollars—if they pay at all. And though that one firm may stop its infringement practices, 10 more will start copying products down the street.

This lax control in a police state amounts to tacit approval. Not being required to pay fair value to the owner of a patent or copyright—whereas we are required by law to do so in the United States—is yet another cost advantage that we are unable to match. The foreign country steals value from the owner of the intellectual property rights on a product because it can make the item in question much more cheaply than the American company that holds the rights. Here in this country we must honor those rights and pay licensing fees. Most big retail chains ignore this issue on the imports they buy, unless it becomes a big news item, calling into question their reputation.

Our entertainment industry, one of the few that shines brightly in these foreign markets, is, not surprisingly, one of the hardest hit by intellectual property theft. It is very common to find copied movies, music, and software all over Asia. Occasional government raids are carried out, but more to placate our complaints than to actually try to stop the practice. The cost to the USA in lost royalties runs into the billions every year.

With patents in particular, ignoring them in manufactured goods can lead to an artificial lowering of the price of a product by 5 to as high as 20 percent, or more. This gives these foreign manufacturers a serious price advantage over small American manufacturers—or, for that matter, manufacturers in other countries that do follow the rules and pay royalties.

In the event that the companies reproducing a patented product, or otherwise violating intellectual property rights, cannot be held liable for their theft, then the government allowing this theft should be. Let the Chinese government be responsible for paying the rights holders retroactively the millions of dollars they deserve, out of its huge surplus. The moment the government there started to truly enforce these rules, most of the copying would stop within a matter of weeks. The fear of the police is that great in China.

GOVERNMENT OWNERSHIP

Government ownership ensures that the wheels of production are oiled in ways that American manufacturers can hardly imagine. It is not just about protection from imports, but also about an active partnership formed to avoid regulations, taxes, and other costs of doing business. The savings in production costs are substantial.

Chinese government-owned firms are never going to lose a bid to a foreign-owned company for any type of construction or other kind of infrastructure project in China. They let foreign companies participate only as minority partners, and only when they need their technology.

Local and provincial officials are very often major owners in firms based in their territories, or that have assets like mines or factories in those territories. That ensures the companies involved get special treatment, in the form of more resources, special treatment by law enforcement, breaks on product or worker safety issues, tax breaks, and protection from lawsuits.

For example, China's coal industry has a horrific safety record, and it is rare to read an in-depth article about an accident or series of accidents in one of its mines where local government ownership is not either openly known or at least implied. For a share in these mines, officials shield the operators from safety regulations and keep the workers in line. Tony Soprano would be proud! True, the coal mine connection gets flushed out more often than most there, because of the high rate of accidents and death, but ownership of shares by local officials in all types of businesses operating in their communities is very common. Direct government ownership, or government officials' ownership of a portion of local suppliers, is a major factor in the protection of those industries and international security.

The Chinese military, too, is a major owner of industry; it even has a controlling interest in companies that have assets here in the United States. They own, for instance, part of a key southern California port, among many other assets in our country. More than just encouraging favoritism, cash they are earning from this involvement supports their weapons procurement for arms that might one day be used against us. It also makes it possible for China's military to upgrade its technology, by repurposing commercial technology for military means.

When I worked at McDonnell Douglas many years ago, before Boeing bought the company, it had delivered technology and tooling to Chinese-based assembly facilities to convince them to buy MD-80 commercial aircraft. China did buy the aircraft, but only after insisting on the addition of high levels of locally procured parts. McDonnell agreed, and soon thereafter key tooling disappeared from the Chinese facility, and clearly went, along with production knowledge, to support China's military development. Though senior management at McDonnell Douglas appeared to have no idea this was about to happen, it seemed apparent that some local Chinese employees and, likely, managers were not only aware of the equipment and knowledge thefts, but probably in on it. Neither the Bush Sr. nor the Clinton administration did anything about these technology leaks.

By virtue of owning so many companies and portions of others, China's military is, in fact, one of the biggest industrial interests in the country. No other major power so intertwines its military with the private sector. Ironically, the military in this pseudo-communist nation is, in itself, quite capitalistic and somewhat independent from Beijing. There is zero doubt leaders are earning a lot of cash from their investments, while also effectively obtaining Western technology. That a Chinese company approaching American or European companies for equipment—which could have military applications, advanced production methods, and know-how—might very well be owned by China's government or military adds another dimension to the challenge Washington and our companies face when dealing with China. Many are not up to handling this level of duplicity. Goodness knows it's often beyond Washington's scope.

GOVERNMENT THAT KEEPS WORKERS IN LINE

A nation that holds itself out to be communist should be all about protecting its workers, right? Not so. Some rules are in place, but the national goal of rapid industrialization takes priority. As I've mentioned, the police are often at the disposal of the factory owners, some of whom are also local officials, to keep workers in line if there is trouble. Certainly anyone who criticizes the government does so at his or her own serious peril. In all my years in Asia, I never found a single person in mainland China willing to criticize the government in any way, unlike in Korea, Japan, Thailand, Singapore, and other nations. The exception to this rule in China is Hong Kong, the former colony the British gave back—some would say, sold out—to China. In Hong Kong, the breath of fresh air blown in by freedom is proving very difficult for Beijing to stifle, so far.

China, which calls itself a "worker's paradise" is more like a nightmare for hundreds of millions. There are unions, yes, but they, too, are controlled by the state.

It is no surprise that products from a police state, where the government is motivated to help and protect the factory owners and rapidly add as much industrial capability as possible, are going to cost less than ones produced in democracies, no matter what other factors are involved. And it's little wonder in a country whose people all fear to criticize the government, and where the government is pushing fast-forward industrialization, that abuses are widespread. Having the government on the side of the factory in all but the most egregious worker abuse issues gives a significant cost advantage to those producing there. A workforce that knows it can strike or take legal action against an employer gets a lot more respect than one that has very few rights. The workers with the state against them may produce more, but they earn a lot less.

Basic human rights cost money.

In this regard, too, Wal-Mart and like companies do not give credit to American manufacturers for paying a living wage and treating their employees right. Worse, the cost advantages they garner from the abusive manufacturing practices in China become a bargaining point, held over the heads of American producers, as the retailers attempt to push their prices lower and lower.

LACK OF ENVIRONMENTAL CONTROLS

A huge cost advantage in many industries is the lack of pollution controls in the third world and, particularly, China. I am not saying that we should lower our standards; I'm simply pointing out that it costs a lot of money to protect the environment appropriately. I have seen firsthand, and learned from the experience of my colleagues who have lived and worked in China, that nations with lower environmental control standards, or that unofficially enforce lower standards through rampant local and provincial corruption, spend a lot less money than we do to make the same items. Depending on how pollution-intensive the production of a given item is, the savings in China could range from a few percent for simple assembly to as much as 40 percent for the production of leathers, chemicals, and certain other products.

I had an American friend who witnessed a worker chrome-plating products at a factory in China, to make them shiny. Chromium is very dangerous to humans and animals, causing very severe health problems. The worker my friend witnessed was dipping products into a vat of chemicals loaded with chromium while wearing only cheap rubber gloves for protection! That is all. There were no safeguards for the worker's arms or face; he was openly exposed to dangerously high levels of chromium every day. To make matters worse, the vat was spilling over the side and draining into a river, where farms just on the other side were growing crops. Not only was everyone in that factory exposed, but also all their neighbors and whoever ate the food grown in the area.

Who tests the food we import from China? Does this situation warrant diligent government workers at every port? It's a trick question, I admit. The answer is no one is testing the food we import from China or other nations.

According to the *Wall Street Journal,* Chinese living near a lead smelting plant rioted and attacked the facility upon learning that *all* the children living in the area had dangerously high levels of lead in their blood.[1] Lead travels from the blood into the brain, especially of children, causing behavioral problems, learning disabilities, and worse. To the parents of the afflicted children, it was obvious that the culprit was the lead smelter in their community; but what about other kids, many miles downstream or downwind who also might have been affected? They might never know that carcinogens or other terrible health risks lurk nearby, simply because producing items cheaply takes precedence over human health and well-being.

These are the types of human-made tragedies that result when corners are cut and safety standards are utterly disregarded. Moreover, the apparent savings discounts the long-term costs to society and the environment imposed by widespread, reckless pollution.

If an American company produces an item that competes with a Chinese product and employs appropriate pollution controls at a cost

20 percent higher, clearly the American company is at an innate disadvantage. For example, if these two companies are competing for business at Wal-Mart, the retailer will focus intently on cost, without consideration of the pollution that may be generated to produce it. The American company may try to shave its profit margin, or do something else to lower its bid to Wal-Mart, but 20 percent is a lot to overcome, even without taking into account the Chinese manufacturer's other unfair advantages. The fact is that as long as a foreign supplier is not polluting so outrageously that people get hurt, hence do not make the news headlines, Wal-Mart has almost no way to accurately verify whether or not the Chinese maker and its many suppliers and subcontractors are adhering to even the most basic environmental control rules. Wal-Mart and the other chain stores will just assume everything is okay, unless they see villagers on television storming the plant that makes their products. Plus, the American manufacturer gets zero credit at Wal-Mart or most other chain stores for "doing the right thing." These chain stores end up pursuing Chinese suppliers that deliver on price and assure their big-name clients that environmental controls are in place and functioning—all at the expense of American suppliers.

If we agree that certain standards are necessary to protect the environment, now and for the future, then we should hold the makers of products that cross our borders to similar standards. To allow this disadvantage to continue hurts American manufacturing and puts our citizens out of work; and in the end, worsening pollution will catch up with us one way or another. Naturally, the people in the community just described in China will bear the brunt of the pollution from that lead smelter, in terms of numbers of children exposed to carcinogens and other poisonous pollutants. However, we cannot be so ignorant as to believe that such pollution does not affect us right here in the USA. Think back to the farm next to the factory spilling chromium: Crops grown in locations like that one, near dangerous factories, are constantly arriving in the United States. Some contain heavy metals and dangerous chemicals; others are carrying bacteria. These poisons also end up in the ocean and, thus, in fish we import. Incinerated pollutants go up in smoke, to the upper atmosphere, which then hovers over the globe before landing wherever the windstreams take it.

Wal-Mart gets its lower prices, but we're the ones who eventually end up paying a higher price, whether it is in the factory down the road that closes, the food we eat, or even the air we and our kids breathe.

CURRENCY MANIPULATION

Overt, or open, trade barriers are easy to criticize. Therefore, countries resort to currency manipulation to give their home manufacturers an advantage while keeping imports from other nations artificially expensive. China is the master of this game. By weakening its currency artificially—40 percent or so according to experts like Bryan Rich—China gains a huge cost advantage over its international rivals.[2]

Manipulating the currency by 40 percent gives Chinese exporters a huge advantage against our companies selling both here and in other nations. Because of this, if, say, a farmer in this country grows grain to sell here or in a country like Japan, he or she is at a distinct disadvantage compared to Chinese farmers. The seed and fertilizers would cost the American farmer and the Chinese farmer roughly the same. I would say that our American farmer's expertise, scale, and commitment make him or her more than a match for Chinese farmers, but the 40 percent difference imposed by the currency manipulation would mean that the Chinese farmers could sell their crops at a price that much lower and still make money. The same is true for any company making anything here that relies on exports from China. I had to laugh when a tariff was imposed on Chinese tires, because at approximately 20 percent, the tariff amounted to only about half the value of their currency manipulation!

Compare Figures 7.1, 7.2, and 7.3 from the brief period between March 2009 and early September 2010 of our dollar versus the Chinese yuan, the European euro, and Japanese yen, based on data from the U.S. Federal Reserve Bank.

As you can see, the figures showing our currency versus the euro and yen indicate normal currency fluctuations, as short- and long-term economic events cause changes over time. The euro starts off getting stronger and stronger as the European economy looks healthier relative to ours; later, it falls off sharply against the dollar as the economic chaos in Greece takes its toll. The Japanese yen steadily

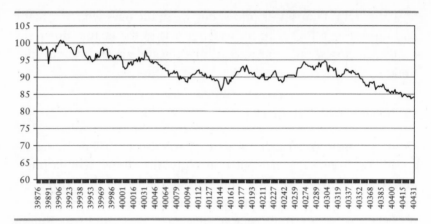

FIGURE 7.1   Japanese Yen to U.S. Dollars
Source: Data from the U.S. Federal Reserve Bank.

appreciates against the dollar, over 15 percent in total in about a year and a half. That means items made in Japan have become 15 percent more expensive relative to the dollar. Toyota and every other Japanese company making products in the country are, therefore, at that much more of a disadvantage during that period.

As Figure 7.3 clearly shows, China's currency moves only very slightly in that same time frame—1 percent—due to the country's

FIGURE 7.2   Euro to U.S. Dollars
Source: Data from the U.S. Federal Reserve Bank.

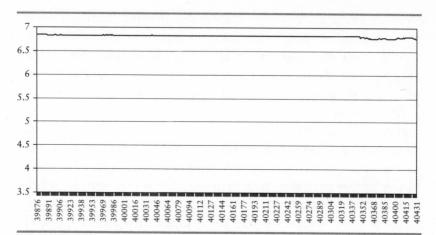

FIGURE 7.3   Chinese Yuan to U.S. Dollars
Source: Data from the U.S. Federal Reserve Bank.

tight controls over it. During this period, the huge trade surplus China had with the United States, coupled with its economic growth versus ours, should have made its currency stronger. Comparing China's economic growth to Japan's, the rate should have appreciated much higher than the yen; that was not the case, however: Japan's appreciated 15 percent to China's 1 percent. This is manipulation on a historic scale to support China's economic growth, at the expense of every other nation.

Occasionally, under some pressure from Washington or the G20, a group of 20 so-called developed nations, China will allow a slight revaluation of its currency. Washington can then declare victory, while Beijing puts on a song and dance to demonstrate it is being flexible. The victory is as false as the flexibility.

Look again at the three figures charting the dollar versus the Chinese yuan and the euro. Note how the dollar versus the euro fluctuates constantly, depending on what is going on in the world politically and trade-wise. The yuan, however, remains nearly flat. That straight line would be absolutely impossible without government intervention on a massive scale.

The fact is that, until the Chinese currency free-floats against every other currency in the world, this game will be stacked, and not only against the dollar but against every other currency in the world.

Consider the Thai: It is completely unfair that their currency moves freely, typically coming to a point of its real value against world currencies, versus the vastly undervalued Chinese currency. So, it is not only American factories that are being forced to close, but those in other nations competing with the Chinese.

What does all this mean to American manufacturers? Experts say that the Chinese currency is 40 percent undervalued, making this the single highest mathematical hurdle our manufacturers have to climb in this unfair competition against China. From my point of view as a former finance executive, with many years of real experience in Asia, this currency factor alone has an impact greater than that of our wage difference here in the USA. The wage difference is a reality, yes, but it's just one factor. Lower worker and product safety standards, freedom from legal or criminal liability, government ownership, patent infringements, and other factors all conspire to make Chinese products seem cheaper to us. As a former finance executive for a major technology company, I have seen the numbers, and am convinced we can make up for the wage difference. As a businessperson with seven years' experience in Asia, I have also seen the extent to which some nations will go to achieve their national goals.

China does incur cost disadvantages, too, but these other benefits are more than enough to make up for them. Here is a list of challenges the Chinese face:

- They are running out of many raw materials, such as ores, timber, energy, and plastics, and these are now being shipped from all over the world to feed China's huge appetite.
- Its workers often are not as efficient or skilled as their American counterparts.
- Electricity is provided inconsistently, and fluctuations in supply are commonplace away from the capital. That wreaks havoc with many manufacturing processes that should not be interrupted.
- The quality of goods from local Chinese suppliers is often poor; and if the final manufacturer is unable to pawn its junk off on its end-use customer, it ends up eating a lot of waste.
- Chinese goods must be shipped all the way from the provinces to the United States.

Product quality is simply better here, and that means lower return rates at the retailers, thereby saving money. These differences are more than enough to offset the impact of the wage difference on production costs. Meaning that we can pay our citizens a good wage and still compete head-on with China.

Today's trade system is rigged against us, and wages are only a small part of the problem. If American manufacturers were given a level field to play on, they would more than be able to make up for the wage difference; they would beat their foreign competitors hands down.

Chapter 8 The Race to the Lowest Common Denominator

Common denominator is a mathematical term used to describe a common multiple of the denominators in a number of fractions. In order to add, for example, 4/8 and 6/12, you have to find a common denominator, a multiple or divisor of both 8 and 12 that will allow you to more easily perform this mathematical function. There are many possible common denominators for 4/8 and 6/12: 24, 48, and 96, just to name a few. But in math, you seek the lowest common denominator to put them in the form that's simpler to work with and understand. In this case, the lowest common denominator is 2. Both 4/8 and 6/12 equal 1/2, a much easier fraction to manipulate.

Common denominator can also be used to describe cultural or economic situations in which the bottom threshold is sought. Here, I use it in the context of major American retail chains taking us down to the lowest common denominator in terms of pricing. They are doing this in two ways. First, they consistently seek out places in the world where products can be purchased or made for the absolute lowest cost, regardless of other factors. Second, major chain stores are looking for the lowest common denominator in the payment for, treatment of, and benefits offered to their employees here in the USA.

The location of cheapest production is not a constant; it can in fact change rapidly. For example, as I mentioned in Chapter 1, a few years ago Thailand became a cheaper place than Vietnam or China to produce women's underwear in bulk. Specifically, the Thai border with Myanmar gave easy access to cheap labor when political troubles there sent tens of thousands of people fleeing to Thailand. However, those refugees failed to make it across and were held just inside the Thai border; now in dire straits, they were compelled to take nearly any job available. Factories popped up like mushrooms, and today much of the women's underwear sold in the United States is produced in this sorrowful place.

The big retail chains, although they are American-owned companies, seem to carry almost nothing but foreign-made products these days. Their choice to do that would seem to defy reason, given that the retailers are putting their own customers in this country out of work, thus eventually gutting their own markets. As the largest agents of cheap, subpar foreign imports into our nation, and leaders of a system in which millions of employees spend their lives working for barely more than minimum wage, America's large retailers are indeed leading the country down a path toward the lowest common denominator.

Wal-Mart, as I pointed out in Chapter 2, is by far the largest importer of Chinese goods to this country, but the other chain stores are following them down that destructive path. They portray themselves as purveyors of a better life, when they are actually undermining our middle class. China could not accomplish its ascendency without the assistance of Wal-Mart and its ilk.

The big retail chains honor the cost god above all others. Their buyers have been trained to search the globe for lower and lower costs, without any consideration of right or wrong, beyond whether it is legal. Buyers after World War II and up until the late 1960s were part of or closely associated with the so-called Greatest Generation,

Americans who helped the country mobilize to defeat the Germans and Japanese, simultaneously. The deployment scale was monumental: Thousands of freedom ships were built and launched to deliver supplies to our troops and allies. "Rosie the Riveter" and millions of patriots like her expanded our industrial base on a scale never seen before in history. Imagine the complexity of moving raw materials and components among thousands of suppliers and manufacturers to produce output at that magnitude. Buyers from that generation naturally looked first to American suppliers. Their shared experience of helping in the struggle to save democracy was a powerful impetus for them to do so.

As the next generation rose through the ranks and started taking over management roles, many treated loyalty to America and its workers and companies as a much lower priority. It marked the start of an age of shortcuts, an age of plastic. "Make it cheap" became the mantra.

HEROES OF OUR USA EFFORT IN THEIR OWN WORDS

America's Oldest Supplier: Holgate Has Been Committed to the USA Since 1789!

Holgate has a tradition, starting back in 1789, of making wood products. That is the year that George Washington became our first president. In 1929, Holgate made its first toys. We continue that tradition today, and believe it is important to carry on the values of past generations and remain true to the standards of 100 percent "Made in the USA." It is important to maintain local jobs and help sustain a local/regional economy. We need to continue to educate consumers to shop for all "Made in USA" products, not just toys.

The key difference is safety and quality. A couple of years ago, the United States was again concerned with lead in children's toys. Holgate maintains long-term relationships with its vendors, most of which are located within a 40-mile radius of our operation. We know the people and companies we are dealing with; this is so critical for keeping our products safe and meeting U.S. toy safety standards. Quality is the other factor. By refusing to outsource, we are able to better control the quality of our toys. American hardwoods are the best in the world for making

(continued)

(*continued*)

toys, and the suppliers we purchase from have used sustainable forestry practices for generations. Their forests are FSC-certified, and they truly work with a natural ecosystem for sustainability. Good wood and local economies: That is what we support by making our toys in the USA.

Holgate toy makers are dedicated to and concerned about making a safe and quality toy. All its employees know that we must perform every day, to earn the respect and trust of consumers. Quality is important, and our employees share in the belief of making the toys in the USA.

There are so many advantages today to manufacturing in the USA. As China grows a middle class, toy components are becoming an undesirable product for them to make. They want high-tech jobs—just like Japan 40 years ago. America offers a workforce and facilities to grow business. However, the federal government needs to relax some of its tax corporate structure to better attract businesses back home.

Holgate is proud of its long tradition, and the fact that we are "Made in the USA."

Before the late 1960s, most imports were brought in because we had no domestic source of a particular resource, like raw rubber. Other imports came from allies, like Britain or Canada, that represented manufacturing values and standards similar to ours, and were generally no threat. As times changed and lessons from history were forgotten, retailers started to seek out cost advantages abroad.

It was the advent of foreign car sales in this country that really opened the door to foreign consumer goods of every type, and made them much more commonly accepted. Japan's efforts to earn foreign currency in dollars at any price finally paid off with the first oil embargo. Because of its limited energy resources and the need to import oil, Japanese cars were necessarily designed to be energy-efficient, whereas American car makers historically valued power over efficiency. Even today, American manufacturers and dealerships promote the power of the engine to get people, especially men, to pay more for cars with engines that have much greater capacity than they need. When I purchased a Saturn LS in 2001, I was shocked to find that the six-cylinder engine was foreign-made, while the four-cylinder version was the American-made one installed in other Saturn models. I had thought all Saturn engines were American-made, so this angered me. Still, the poor salesman came on strong about how "bigger engines are for real men and smaller engines are for women." He probably still remembers my irate reaction to that. Needless to say, I bought the version with the American-made engine.

World War II taught Japan important economic lessons, and they learned them well. The money they earned was wisely reinvested, again and again, in factories, workers, quality, and technology—until a few years ago, when companies like Toyota peaked. When the oil embargo went into effect in the early 1970s, the Japanese were perfectly placed to take advantage with their more fuel-efficient car lineup. Only now, 30-plus years later, are American car companies addressing the fuel efficiency issue head-on. Had we addressed this 30, or even 20, years ago, we could have pushed the Japanese import invasion back into the Pacific, and the Big Three USA car makers would be vastly better off today.

The widespread acceptance of foreign cars in this country made it easier for retailers like Wal-Mart to ease more and more foreign goods into their stores, eventually turning themselves into gigantic import machines. That practice doesn't sit well with many Americans when it's presented to them directly; but in everyday life, many of us simply don't give it any thought. And as long as the majority of people don't make a conscious decision to take a stand against this pattern, the big retail chains will continue to undermine what little industry we have left. Make no mistake, these retailers are powerful; but that arrogance is also their weakness, a chink in their armor, that makes it possible for their customers to force a change.

In the wake of the widespread acceptance of foreign-made automobiles, times began changing for the worse. Big retailers actively began seeking out more and more undesirable locations in which to have their items made, because doing so enabled cheaper production of goods. It wasn't always that way. Many American retailers—even some of the worst offenders today—have proud histories.

Wal-Mart founder Sam Walton brought a mix of heartfelt patriotism and marketing savvy to his company. Under his direction, the company was steadfast in its attempt to buy American-made goods, even as other retailers were turning to cheaper goods manufactured in police states around the world. Sadly, when Walton learned he had terminal cancer, and started to take himself out of the picture, the retailer's new leader, David Glass,[1] completely abandoned what was left of the corporate preference for American-made goods and instead pushed into overdrive an agenda of seeking out ultracheap sources abroad, with no questions asked about local conditions. Wal-Mart's ascendency went hand in hand with the surge in Chinese imports. The two grew together on an unprecedented scale. Over time, Wal-Mart wore down the bias of its customer base to buy American-made goods by encouraging them to pay less and less attention to country of origin. Though it seems that a majority of American consumers are sympathetic to the "Made in USA" cause, many are easily distracted by advertising, price comparisons, and other strategies employed by the large retail chains. Most do not bother to read labels.

Lands' End underwent a similar transformation. Recall my conversation with one of the company's buyers in Chapter 7. That experience was particularly disheartening because under the leadership of the company's founder, Gary Comer,[2] Lands' End had made a commitment to American-made goods, and all that comes with them. That's all changed; it is very rare to find any American-made products in its catalog today.

I occasionally get calls from employees of Wal-Mart and other big chain stores who privately applaud our efforts to support American manufacturing; but they dare not say anything at work for fear of losing their jobs. One from Sears told us he was terminated after honestly answering a customer question about where to buy American-made products within earshot of a manager. Behind closed doors, Wal-Mart employees will complain that their pay is poor, and that they can't make enough to raise their kids; some can't afford Wal-Mart's expensive medical insurance. Sadly, they say they feel they have no choice and must take what they can get.

That kind of job isn't what most of us want for ourselves or would wish for our own kids, yet many people blindly shop at such stores without considering the system they're supporting. Wal-Mart is now the biggest private employer in this country. There is a military term for soldiers who, though injured, are able to move away from the front on their own: They are the "walking wounded." Many employees of Wal-Mart and similar retailers become a sort of "working wounded," moving forward from day to day but unable to make enough to better themselves or fully provide for their families without government help. These are the workers entirely ignored by those who say such things as, "It's all a matter of personal choice; anyone who chooses to work hard can get ahead. Millions of people are working hard every day yet falling further behind; and that number will only increase as more and more quality jobs are replaced with positions like Wal-Mart clerk, greeter, and parking lot attendant.

One retail employee I spoke with while looking for American-made products at the store where he worked told me no one cares about goods being made in this country anymore. A tall guy, in his early thirties and wearing a wedding ring, he looked a bit like a young Tom Selleck. Without wanting to pry, but wanting to understand his situation, I asked him how much he makes. He looked down at me and answered with pride, "I am a supervisor now, so I make $10.50 an hour." On a hunch, I next asked, "How much does your father make at the plant?" He again replied without hesitation: "He does real well; $30 an hour before benefits and overtime." I just nodded; I did not have to say anymore. His eyes had already changed, even misting up a bit, as he looked away, I imagined into a hard future. He was a hard worker and probably had more education than his father, yet with the economy the way it is today in this country, he has many fewer opportunities than his father did. His parents built a nation and were rewarded for it. They probably made enough to buy a house, raise their family, maybe even take a vacation now and then, and still be able to save a bit. Past generations in this country believed their children would have more than they did; not anymore. This is a direct result of our industry leaving these shores, leaving the USA because Wal-Mart and other retail chains allow it—worse, they encourage it.

It used to be that American corporations had to buy, if not from other democracies, then at least from nations friendly to the United States. Today, the only nations that are off-limits are those we have sanctions against. Today's retailers take no responsibility for the factors that make it possible for foreign manufacturing to quote them such low prices, like heavy pollution, minimal workers' rights, lower product safety standards, and so on.

The manufacturers that take advantage of unstable political climates, police corruption, and low wages to reduce their production costs, are, along with Wal-Mart and the other big manufacturers, playing a shell game with the third world and developing nations to squeeze out those last few pennies. They are also squeezing those desperate enough to work at their stores in this country. I am not belittling those who have to work for these companies to scratch out a living, but very few of these folks would wish such jobs upon their own children for the long term.

If the pay is so low and the benefits so few that it is just about impossible to adequately support a family, even with both parents working, the American dream is dying. When even those working full-time need welfare benefits to help pay for their kids' medical care, something is wrong. I'm not talking about part-time jobs one spouse takes to subsidize the household income. The employees at these stores—"associates," as Wal-Mart calls them—are often the primary wage earners in their households; sometimes, they are the only wage earners. If a good manufacturing job became available, however hard, paying $25-plus an hour with good benefits, many would leap at the opportunity. The desperation that drives many Americans to work at these big retail chains, particularly Wal-Mart, gives these companies power over these folks who need to feed their kids and pay their bills. Management knows the situation many of their employees are in, and knows, too, that is what prevents them from demanding higher wages and better conditions.

Fear and arrogance give management teams at such companies the power to drive wages lower and lower, and to seek out minimal prices for products around the world without concern for what happens at the American factories where their own customers work, and without regard for the truth about that foreign factory's safety or pollution standards. Greed drives them to aim for the lowest common denominators in both products and people. Sam Walton, the founder of Wal-Mart, was a true American in many ways, and did what he could to keep production in this country. Unfortunately, Wal-Mart's commitment to the USA died with him, and we are all the poorer for it.

It's time to put an end to this cycle. Wal-Mart and the large retail chains are powerful, but we are far from powerless. They are determined to push the envelope to arrive at the lowest common denominator for products and employees, but we have the ultimate authority: We decide where we shop. Don't misunderstand: I am not telling anyone where they should or should not buy something new for their kids. The cycle put into motion by these large-scale, low-paying employers make the economic realities difficult for too many Americans. But those of us who do have a choice should take our dollars elsewhere. Even those of us on tight budgets can make small changes that make a difference.

Start by thinking about the stores where you shop. Did Retailer X cause a local company to close in order to get low, low prices? If so, don't shop there. Did Retailer Y treat someone you know in an abusive way? Shop elsewhere. We each hold the real power, and we can use it to send messages, both positive and negative. Does Retailer Z treat you, its employees, and its suppliers with respect? Pay a living wage? Add value to the communities where it does business? That sounds like one of the few remaining independent, family-owned businesses in this country. Their owners raised their kids in their communities. They have known their employees for decades. They never forget how important their customers are. The trouble is, they have been slammed on every front; the big chains have undercut every product category in a big way.

It is difficult, for example, to succeed as an independent pharmacist in a town with a Wal-Mart that has a pharmacy, where drugs are sold for lower prices. Wal-Mart often uses its pharmacies as a way to get customers into the store, where they will wander around while waiting for their prescriptions to be filled. Naturally, most of these people end up shopping. That means the large retailer is willing to lose money on its pharmacy in order to draw in that business. It is very hard for an independent, local pharmacist to survive when the Wal-Mart price for most medications is below the local pharmacist's cost. In a sense, Wal-Mart is using low-priced medications as a gimmick or shell game to raise sales elsewhere in its stores. For that independent pharmacist, it may have been his livelihood, built through helping his community for 20 years. He was regarded by the townspeople as a real expert, someone they could come to with questions, someone who knew them and their medical histories, someone who cared about them, and sponsored their kids' little league teams. Now, at the big-box retailer pharmacy, a stranger counts out their pills, and if they have a question, just reads the label to them.

I encourage those of us who can afford it to shop at locally owned stores and buy American-made products. If we have to drive a bit farther to do so, we should do it. Rewarding their loyalty to us in this way pays off manyfold, and goes a long way toward nurturing and ensuring the future of our communities. Remember, every choice counts. If you can't afford to switch all of your patronage to local retailers and American-made goods, figure out what you can change. Consider whether the superior quality and durability of American-made goods might actually make it cost-effective to buy a more expensive American-made item, knowing that it will last longer.

Let those who do not care patronize the Mega-Mart and be its shopping drones, or sheep. Those of us who know better will be strong. We know things can be different. We will be smart and think about choices and alternatives. We won't look just at the price tag, but count the real cost to our society. We will take real action based on the facts; we won't just sit on our butts.

To inspire you to take action, imagine Wal-Mart's nightmare: Customers who recognize that things can and should be better, who actually consider superior alternatives, and who have the gumption to drive on past their big parking lots in search of better.

Together, we can stop the slide to the lowest common denominator, both overseas and right here in the USA.

Three

Rebuilding American Manufacturing

Chapter 9 The American Advantage

It seems like China has all the cost advantages: low labor costs, low product safety and worker safety costs, much lower environmental costs, currency manipulation, and others. But don't count the USA out yet. Our country has a lot of strengths and advantages, too.

It is easy to lose sight of our many strengths and get discouraged about our nation's future; but keep the faith, and remember that we are superior in many ways that other nations cannot begin to compete with.

OUR PEOPLE

Our biggest advantage stems from one thing: the caliber of our people.

This unique country was created by our forefathers based not on race or creed, but on a set of ideas and beliefs. It was intended to be something new, a society that took the best from the past and rejected the unfair biases of the old world. No longer would men and women be segregated into certain groups or classes; they would have the opportunity to earn their own way.

That new world was populated by immigrants and the descendants of immigrants. Much of the world looks down on immigrants, as little better than dirty refugees; but in this country, it is a badge of honor. When I lived in Japan, I was treated well as a Westerner and "guest worker," who would be leaving after a few years; but it was easy to see that Koreans and Chinese who live there occupy the lowest rung on the cultural ladder, even those who achieve financial success. In the United States, those same immigrants would likely carry the special spark common to those who uproot their lives and travel to live in this country—who are determined to better their lives. Many of our customers at MadeinUSAForever.com tell us they are immigrants, and readily share their pride in their adopted nation, along with their deep concern for the USA and its future. Too bad that many of those whose families have been here for many generations seem to need to be reminded of what freedom is really about.

With people descended from virtually every country around the globe and forged into one society, we have created the most diverse nation the world has ever known. That diversity means we have the strength, background, talent, and experience from all those peoples at our disposal. We have the power to renew our country and rise to new heights.

Visualize for a moment the dawn rising over the East Coast, through the trees and mountains, spreading golden light to each and every community and home. The sunlight keeps spreading west, taking some hours to touch the rest of our great nation, until finally we are all bathed in its warmth, together as one nation, one people. That new dawn awakens a great people; hundreds of millions rise to greet a new day; our strength awakens with each person. What if each of us asked, "Will I make the USA better in some small way today?" What if we stood together in our millions to ask that question today, as we did during World War II, or the 1960s, when we made it to the moon?

An America whose people are united in a common goal shines as bright as dawn's new light. Unlike the citizens of other countries who may be compelled by tradition or force, our people are free to choose to unite in a common purpose. We are free to come together in support of an idea, as one, because of what we believe, rather than our race, gender, or background or some other factor beyond our control.

HEROES OF OUR USA EFFORT IN THEIR OWN WORDS

Beating the Chinese at Their Own Game—Battle Lake Outdoors

There is a perception globally that products made in the USA are of high quality, made by highly skilled workers. This is particularly true in our industry. We receive inquiries regularly from both domestic and foreign companies to acquire our USA-made products because of the quality they have been able to find only in this country. This gives us the privilege of providing jobs to Americans, especially in our small Midwestern town, and enables us to take a part in strengthening the economy of the United States.

Producing our goods gives us the ability to provide a level of service to our customers that we would not be able to accommodate if we produced items abroad. We are able to work directly with our customers in designing new products; monitor the quality of the products and the conditions under which they are made, firsthand; and respond quickly to the needs of our customers.

We believe we have high-quality workers in the USA. People here have many opportunities and choices about education, jobs, and location that do not exist everywhere in the world. This encourages an environment where workers can choose work they enjoy, which in turn promotes pride in their work and better performance. Employers, in turn, can choose educated, skilled workers, who provide quality products and services.

Having manufacturing companies here in the USA is an important part of keeping the economy strong, by providing jobs to American citizens, keeping capitalism strong, and helping to maintain a well-rounded industry base in our country. Manufacturing products involves such a wide use of products, services, skills, and education that manufacturing companies have a lot to offer, and impact every location they are in. We have highly skilled workers, as well as high-quality product and services in the USA. In our experience, customers seek that out and are willing to pay for it.

With the right motivation, that diverse body of people, united, is our key strength, one that no other nation can match. Many other countries were formed long ago by tribes marauding their way across physical boundaries, and are held together by common experience in developed nations and force in much of the rest of world. Low-cost competition emerges in countries where force rules and/or extreme poverty is prevalent. Workers in such places can be motivated for a while by money or fear, but in the long run they will never be a match for a motivated free people.

As I've said, I have been around the world and lived in Asia, twice, for a total of seven years, and have never seen anyone work harder than a motivated American. We see examples of this every day, in the small business owner who works 60-plus hours a week, often without pay; in the college student who works his or her way through school; in the truck driver who covers hundreds of miles overnight. The list goes on and on. When employees have the chance to succeed, they go above and beyond, doing whatever it takes to make things better for themselves and their families. The ripple effect of that investment goes far beyond the worker and his or her family; given the chance, dedicated employees also make things better for their employers and our nation as a whole.

The question is not whether we can reclaim the motivation to meet our future goals, but how and when. When the majority awakens from this stupor we are in currently, we will have passed the hardest test; we will break the mental chains that tie us to the false perception that decline is inevitable.

Just watch us when we have a goal in our hearts. We will move mountains.

Perhaps some folks have drifted away from this can-do attitude, after listening to the propaganda of politicians or becoming discouraged by current economic conditions. But our nation's ideals are still there, beneath the surface, waiting to lay the foundation of our future. That foundation may be covered up or obscured temporarily, but that doesn't change the fact that core ideals are ingrained in every American. Remember Rosie the Riveter and the millions of others like her who did so much to help us win World War II? Her spirit is still among us, if we just look.

This shadow, or funk, that afflicts us now is not more powerful than we are. It can be beaten, on an individual and national basis, by being proactive. Taking a stand as individuals empowers each of us and can dispel the sense of despair; it makes a real difference for us, one by one and collectively as a nation. The action you take and the change you make in your attitude will spread to those around you, and around them, and so on. A thousand such people can take a stand. A million can effect real change. A nation of empowered people can alter history.

The effort to bring manufacturing back to the United States is already gaining ground. You may have seen advertisements recently in which sellers make a point of letting you know that their goods are made in the USA. The advertising campaign built around the 2011 Jeep Grand Cherokee, for example, focuses heavily on the fact that the vehicle was "imagined, drawn, carved, stamped, hewn, and forged here in America." It's great news that American workers are designing, creating, and constructing that vehicle; but what may be even better news is that Jeep is building a major ad campaign around that image. Jeep's marketing strategy is a clear indication that companies are hearing the voices of those who are demanding American-made goods, and that major corporations doing business in this country realize that buying American is important to many of us. Just as more and more grocers have started carrying organic food in response to consumer demand, who let them know they would patronize other shops if necessary, to find it, so large retailers will bend to our will once they realize we will go elsewhere to find American-made goods. It appears that they are beginning to get that message. It's up to us to build on and reinforce that momentum now, while we have their attention.

You have probably noticed by now that I have not given you specifics about what you can and should do personally to support this effort. Part of the privilege of being an American is that you are free to decide what inspires you; no one can know this other than you. We are a nation of innovators, entrepreneurs, and explorers, who find a way to do what needs to be done. Reaching inside for courage, and acting on issues great and small, are the keys to taking this power to the next level. An American, in a nutshell, is a free person who decides for him- or herself. If the efforts of a few are a song, imagine the symphony when millions sing their tune!

ENTREPRENEURIAL OPPORTUNITIES

An American attempting to launch a business anywhere else in the world would likely be in for a rude awakening. What takes hours here takes months in many nations. According to DoingBusiness.org, it takes 6 days to found a business in the United States, versus 38 days in China and 141 days in Venezuela.[1] It took me just a few days to found MadeinUSAForever.com here in the States.

The obstacles aren't all erected by government; there are cultural barriers as well. Few nations are as open as ours to having friends and family members start a business. In America, we recognize that today's entrepreneurs could be tomorrow's Steve Jobs, Bill Gates, Ross Perot, Mary Kay Ash, Roger Penske, Henry Ford, or John D. Rockefeller. Such entrepreneurs endure long days and nights, and headache after headache, determined to create something special—not unlike an artist. Many fail in their efforts. Few make it really big, but all strengthen our nation, and along the way learn important lessons that can immediately be applied to other aspects of their lives and their next ventures. They, with their passion and "outside-the-box" thinking, are a powerful engine that will drive our economy and bring new things to life. A few of their ideas and innovations will grow into companies that make a real impact. For example, years ago, it was Polaroid and Xerox; today, it is Apple and Intel. The dreamers of tomorrow will set in motion future trends we cannot begin to imagine today.

Encourage them when you can. I know firsthand how difficult such an undertaking can be. Working up the gumption to throw off the corporate security blanket and found MadeinUSAForever.com was not easy for me. A big company provides a sense of security (many times, false), but also can hold one back, on many levels. Starting a company taught me a thousand lessons I never learned in all of my years working for big companies.

Launching a business also stretches a person's capabilities and finances to the limit, with new stresses emerging at each step along the way. Every problem at work, like a computer crash or a shipping glitch, ultimately is up to the entrepreneur to solve. Why do it? Why create something new? Why not live a less stressful life among the crowd? There are probably as many reasons as there are entrepreneurs. Some prefer to make their own rules; others do not want to waste their lives in a cubicle; still others seek ownership of—or at least credit for—their ideas. These men and women choose to try to develop something special over taking the path of least resistance.

These determined souls are very important to our economy. According to the Small Business Administration (SBA), small businesses create over 60 percent of new jobs and employ over half the private sector workers in our entire nation.[2] That is a powerful engine driving our economy. However, though we still encourage folks to start businesses at a rate much higher than most nations, we have trended away from that in this era of big government, and when retail chain stores like Wal-Mart are willing to make any compromise for the lowest possible price. Moving back toward encouraging folks to follow their dreams in this way will be crucial to our future. Remember, millions of jobs are created by entrepreneurs, so empowering them is vital to our renewal as a nation.

ABILITY TO RESPOND QUICKLY TO THE DOMESTIC MARKET

Today and for the foreseeable future, the United States is the premium world market for goods. Toyota sells more cars here than in Japan, and makes more profit per car from those they sell here.

No one is closer to our consumers, or better understands their tastes, than we are, ourselves. Producing locally allows us to produce what our customers want and get it to them within days, whereas it takes months to ship goods from China, door to door. We are just beginning to understand the magnitude of the environmental impact caused by bringing boatloads of cheap goods over here from the other side of the planet. Those giant cargo container ships burn huge amounts of fossil fuels; they pollute their way here full, and back to China nearly empty—almost entirely unregulated until very recently, according to *The Guardian*:[3]

> Confidential data from maritime industry insiders based on engine size and the quality of fuel typically used by ships and cars shows that just 15 of the world's biggest ships may now emit as much pollution as all the world's 760m cars. Low-grade ship bunker fuel (or fuel oil) has up to 2,000 times the sulphur content of diesel fuel used in U.S. and European automobiles.

Compare that process with local manufacturing. Not only can local manufacturers get customers what they want when they want it, but the amount of energy used to put it in their hands amounts to just a tiny fraction of the total burned by shipping imports. As energy prices rise, making products nearer their markets just makes good economic sense. As important, from the perspective of our nation's future, it adds to our self-sufficiency, where any improvement over today's trade situation is welcome. Making something in Asia and shipping it here uses substantially more of the globe's limited fossil fuel energy than producing and selling it locally. Since an increasing amount of the oil we use comes from nations that are not our friends, using less of it is not only cheaper, but deprives them of our money. Not to mention that burning less energy overall reduces pollution.

Having factories near their customers also enables manufacturers to ensure that product safety and worker conditions meet or exceed acceptable standards. By allowing contractors abroad to make our products, we surrender all control over these important issues. No company that has turned its manufacturing over to foreign contractors is able to truly understand what is going on over there.

Keeping manufacturing on our shores also allows for quick alterations or customization, to adjust to rapidly changing customer needs and requirements. The United States is the market center for so many products; it makes complete sense that it should be the center of production, as well.

As you can see, the advantages to bringing manufacturing back to its most important market are manifold.

A PLACE WORTH RAISING YOUR FAMILY

Safety and security in this country are essential for the people living here, and critical for the health of our economy. The vast majority of our country is safe, but the pockets where that's not the case tell a different economic tale. Decayed urban or rural centers that are more at risk from crime and abandonment are less attractive to investment by the private sector because the emotional and cash costs of doing business in those areas is higher. For example, I considered opening my new business in Long Beach or Riverside, California, to take advantage of the lower rents there, but discovered that the security issues at the time in those locations outweighed the savings. I had to make another choice, in spite of sympathizing with their situation.

Thanks to our cultural values, the United States is, overall, a very safe place to live, compared with other nations—particularly to the low-cost production nations. Kidnapping has become a way of life in Mexico and the Philippines. The perpetrators may net huge returns, but the risk costs to those societies add up to untold billions in developmental investment. During my time in Asia, I did not see a single example of investment in the Philippines, except when it was required in order to sell to that small market. It was nearly the only nation in Asia where I would not travel outside the hotel without security. Complicating the problem is that at the same time international money does not flow *into* the country, billions earned by locals unofficially flow *out* to banks in Singapore and other locations outside the Philippines. The better security in Singapore makes it a safe place to park money and do business.

My former company, Western Digital, suffered losses from organized theft at its Malaysia facility, in transport to the airport, at the airport itself, and for other reasons. Those losses were small in the grand scheme of things, but enough to be noticeable, and recognized as a cost of doing business there.

Our nation does not have a perfect security record, but it is at a much higher level here than anywhere in the third world, and this is definitely an important advantage.

LACK OF CORRUPTION

There is some government corruption here in the United States; small scandals erupt from time to time over, for example, an official accepting payoffs for favors. But these make up a tiny fraction of what occurs regularly in many nations around the world. Corruption is a serious problem in most Asian nations, where government favors are definitely for sale. As I've mentioned before, in China, local government officials are said to often be part owners of businesses they are charged with overseeing. In addition to the worker safety and environmental issues I've already described, this type of conflict of interest leads to poor-quality building, road construction, and product manufacture. I was astounded to see brand-new buildings in Beijing where the concrete on the inside was already crumbling because low-quality materials had been used. The shoddy quality strongly implied that local building inspectors had been bribed. You would never see conditions like this in the United States or Japan, where it would be more difficult to overlook such issues.

Corruption is a high cost of doing business in many places in the world. Even citizens of some European countries must pay small bribes just to get everyday things done, and the situation is considerably worse in the developing world. There is a perception that corruption gets cleaned up as a nation develops, but such habits are ingrained, going back for generations. Also, as the businesspeople in these nations grow richer, civil servant and police wages often do not keep up, not even with the cost of living. The pressure and temptation to accept—or demand—envelopes filled with money rises.

My estimate, based on my experience working in Asia, puts the monetary cost of doing business in a somewhat corrupt culture at about 20 percent higher than in a more honest culture. And that doesn't even take into consideration the lower quality of life. Malaysia, Singapore, and the Philippines all started out roughly equally poor after World War II. The Philippines even had the advantage of receiving a massive amount of aid from the United States; but as the most generally corrupt of the three, it now lags a distant third, from an economic perspective. For relatively small nations, Malaysia and the Philippines both have considerable natural resources. Of the two, Malaysia's level of corruption, though notable, has generally been of a less serious nature than in the Philippines. Nonetheless, Malaysia's growth and modernization has been impressive. Singapore, in contrast, has no natural resources other than its excellent port and hard-working population, and is remarkably free of government corruption. It is little wonder that Singapore's development today is vastly beyond that of the Philippines, Malaysia, and most other nations in the region.

The great majority of the United States enjoys that same privilege, regardless of what many popular television series might have you believe; corruption is comparatively slight in this country. Absence of corruption not only lowers costs, but improves quality of life. That said, we must remain vigilant, and nurture our culture's intolerance for corruption, to sustain and grow this advantage of civility and stability, so important in a chaotic world. Both economic good times and bad times foster extremes that can breed corruption, and even shade as heroic behavior that needs to be addressed. For example, cocaine seemed to be presented in the media as "cool" for a brief time during the economic boom of the 1980s. Quantities of drugs and the money spent on them could not have changed hands without local police knowing. Thankfully, society typically turns against such behavior; but until it does, society pays a huge cost.

I founded a company here in the United States and have not paid a single bribe, not since day one. That would be unheard of in most other nations I have worked in. The freedom to work in such an environment is definitely an advantage.

INFRASTRUCTURE

Though our infrastructure does face challenges in some states and cities, most of our frameworks and systems are of much higher quality than in most other nations. Where other nations struggle just to build an infrastructure, ours is already in place. Trying to move raw materials or finished goods around in a large part of the world is, simply, not doable—not without delays, expenses, and damage.

Furthermore, maintaining such a large infrastructure is much less problematic and expensive than building a new one. That translates to: savings in the cost of moving raw materials and finished goods, shorter delivery times, and fewer losses from damage in transport, versus developing nations.

It isn't only developing nations that are at a disadvantage to the United States. In college, I had an argument with a German who was convinced that Europe's infrastructure was much more sound than ours. Having just driven from near Tampa to Chicago in about 18 hours, I asked him if the same would have been possible from Lisbon to Berlin. He just glared at me.

Having a reliable infrastructure in place is a major benefit, enabling us to produce and move goods efficiently and cost-effectively.

EDUCATED WORKFORCE AND CUSTOMERS

Our educational system is in need of reform, true, but still the majority of our workers and customers are highly literate and well informed. It is rare to meet someone in the United States who is completely illiterate. Sure, Norway has better math scores than we do, but who cares? The real threat to our manufacturing comes not from Norwegians, but from low-cost nations where there are serious literacy issues.

Nearly every worker here can read a user's manual well enough to understand what he or she needs to do to keep things running. In many cultures, even basic malfunctions cause work stoppages. Worse, machine maintenance simply goes undone. It is amazing how fast a foreign facility will have trouble when its workers are not capable of fixing things, and the engineers who are don't believe in getting their hands dirty. I had a friend who found himself at an international oil refinery that was experiencing a mechanical breakdown. The workers dared not touch the machinery, and the engineers all sat in the control room looking at drawings. Where could the problem be? He walked around, turned a few valves, and, sure enough, fixed the problem.

Yes, we need to improve the effectiveness and raise the caliber of our education and skills development systems, to ensure that we are preparing highly skilled workers, like engineers, in sufficient quantity to meet future growth needs; nevertheless, our educational system is remarkable compared to that of most of our key competitors. It is to American universities that the best researchers in the world come to study. According to *The Times Higher Education's* 2010–2011 listing of the 200 top universities, 15 of the top 20 were American schools.[4]

TRADITION OF MANUFACTURING

Let's face it: The United States practically invented mass assembly manufacturing. Mercedes may have made the first modern self-propelled automobile, but it was Henry Ford who showed them how to turn out cars en masse instead of one at a time. The assembly line and interchangeability of parts in the factory changed the workplace forever, allowing manufacturing on a scale of millions. Instead of a few craftsmen building something over days or months, hundreds of people could build hundreds of thousands of items in much shorter time frames.

The American tradition of manufacturing reaches back to our founding fathers. Americans have always been blessed with a can-do mentality; it is as much a part of our cultural DNA as baseball and apple pie. It has only been very recently that moving paper around came to be treated as viable work. Not so very long ago, a man could have said he worked at GE, and folks would have been excited to hear that, and asked what the company made. That may not be so true at GE anymore, but there are plenty of others where it still is. Manufacturing at a well-managed and maintained company is still a place to make good wages, particularly compared with the vast majority of service industry jobs. The Bureau of Labor Statistic data referenced in Chapter 4 shows that the average service wage per hour, including benefits, is half that of jobs in the manufacturing field.

One of America's goals has to be to make manufacturing jobs "cool" again for young people. More, we should ensure they will be well rewarded wage- and benefit-wise for taking these jobs. For their part, they should be smart, flexible, and willing to do stints in other states, if necessary. We are already developing workers who are smart, hardworking, and dedicated to fill positions in the new type of manufacturing. They can fix an advanced machine or run a computer just as easily as work a 12-hour shift. These are workers of every age; they are curious, intelligent, and have a need to create.

"Doers" like these young men and women will add vastly greater value to our culture than paper-pushers. They will want tangible evidence of what they are creating, and to know it has meaning. For these entrepreneurs, it will not be as much about management versus worker, not about a manager trying to fit a "round" employee into a square peg. Today, a manager might be talking to a human resources employee, but he would rather be out welding, like he used to.

Though some misguided businesses and chain stores have done their best to shut down American manufacturing, it is in our nation's blood, and cannot be dismissed so lightly.

We are Americans, and we make things.

BUSINESS-FRIENDLY CULTURE

The USA is one of the most business-friendly nations on earth, as long as the company is doing the right thing. This is important, as many cultures are hostile to business in general, always assuming the worst. Unlike most Americans, many Europeans believe that wealth cannot be created; rather, that it can only be taken or transferred from one individual to another. Thus, in their opinion, wealthy people are those who have been most successful at taking it from someone else. Such thinking only invites the government in to raise taxes, until everyone is poorer.

Of course, we have corporate cannibals here, too, that bear watching. But making money itself is not suspect; indeed, the concept is as American as the USA itself. (Did you know that the dollar sign is actually a combination of "U" and "S"?) We believe, generally, that if folks work hard and run successful businesses that add value to our culture, they should be rewarded for their efforts—efforts that have not taken wealth from someone else, but created value where there was none before.

There needs to a balance between too little and too much respect for money. That balance shifts over time, but is often just where it needs to be to maintain a system that allows for economic growth but without going over the edge. A healthy respect for wealth built over time is a positive for our culture. Conversely, worshipping instant wealth and fame are not; rather, they are sure signs of an over-stimulated economy.

Some states are more open to manufacturing than others, but in general, compared to what I have seen abroad, our nation is very friendly to business.

NATURAL RESOURCES

We still have vast quantities of untapped natural resources in this country, with the exception of oil and a few minerals. Our government owns a third of our land, mainly in the mountainous West and Alaska. Opening up more of these resources for utilization would create jobs and increase our security—as long as we do it in a way that does not damage our national parks or wilderness heritage.

It has to be done safely and cleanly, but it can be done.

LEGAL IMMIGRATION

We are a nation of immigrants and their descendants. Legal immigrants are the backbone of our nation's workforce. They bring to this country their dreams, knowledge, and work ethic, which are nothing short of breathtaking! They start businesses, they study hard, they send their kids to school, they obey the law, they provide a flexible workforce, and they make valuable contributions to our society. They come here to make a better life for themselves and their families, bringing with them the best of their foreign cultures and adding it our own. Here, they have opportunities; in their homelands they had none.

As a nation we are proud of our immigrant heritage. Few other nations are as open to immigrants of any ethnicity. Take a look at the very strict immigration laws in Japan, which are enforced in spite of the country's serious aging issue, which an influx of immigrants could help. Mexico, which always pressures the United States to ease immigration laws, is itself closed to immigrants—particularly, and ironically, from south of its own border.

Some of the USA's best and brightest minds have been immigrants— Albert Einstein, Alexander Graham Bell, Andrew Grove, Liz Claiborne, John Shalikashvili, Andrew Carnegie, and countless others.

BECAUSE WE CAN

After all my travels and years living abroad, I can say without hesitation I have never known a people quite like the Americans. We know how to turn dreams into reality; we live in a country where anyone can succeed, no matter how modest his or her upbringing; we try to spread justice and freedom to other peoples; we are the only nation to put a man on the moon.

In short, I am confident we will meet the coming challenges and come out stronger, better, and smarter from the effort. We have only to choose that path.

The United States of America: The nation that makes it happen.

Chapter 10 What Can Our People Do?

How do we get the USA back to greatness?

The choice is ours.

The ultimate threat to democracy and our way of life does not come from China or Islam, but from apathy. Do we still care? Are we willing to put an idea into action? Will we make our stand as a people, united?

Every day, we send a message about what is important to us in what we buy and our commitment to the ideas we believe in. Whether we choose consciously or simply opt for the easiest and most obvious solution, we vote with our dollars every time we buy something. Every choice determines the kind of life we will lead, whether we will reach for excellence or settle for apathy. To take a stand when most dare not is the definition of bravery.

The situation may seem too big or complex for an individual to have an impact, but that's a misperception—one that prevents too many good people from taking action. We each can make a real difference. If every adult in this country made the commitment to buy one $30 American-made product per month, instead of its foreign version, we would directly create 500,000 jobs here in the USA. And, as I've already explained, those production jobs would lead to additional jobs at suppliers, transporters, and other companies that support the manufacturing and sales processes.

Such a personal action is meaningful, and not as difficult as many people seem to believe. All that's necessary is to read a label here and there, and show your preference for items made by our fellow citizens. If the store you're in does not carry American-made products, tell the manager why you are leaving before you head to the next one. If the next store does not have what you are looking for, either, go to MadeinUSAForever.com. I created this company not just as a retail site, but as a resource where you can easily research products made in the USA. You are welcome to use it as a free information resource. You might be surprised by what you find there, and how low the prices for American-made products can be.

For example, I took a peek inside a Sears recently, where I saw a pair of men's Levi's for $44. More distressing than the price was seeing that they were made in China! Levi's, Lee, and even Wrangler have sold us out and moved production of this American apparel icon to foreign countries. To add insult to injury, these companies clearly don't pass their savings along to their consumers after taking advantage of cheap foreign wages; in many cases, they actually raise prices! Had they spent just a few seconds on MadeinUSAForever.com, they would have learned that awesome American-made jeans are available for around $35. These are 100 percent made in the USA, from the cotton to the stitching, adding value and employing Americans every step of the way.

Obviously, it *is* possible to manufacture competitively within the USA, and to beat cheap overseas producers at their own game. Unfortunately, too many Americans today simply accept as fact that American-made goods are prohibitively expensive or too hard to find, and so never go looking for those options.

When it comes to how important it is for us as individuals to buy American-made goods and support U.S. manufacturing, we tend to break down into four groups:

- Those who already stand with us.
- Those who are sympathetic, but not really thinking actively about the issue currently.
- Those who are unaware and have little opinion, but could become sympathetic.
- Those who do not, and will never, care, or who would rather support imports.

We must raise awareness of the grave importance of this issue to those among the sympathetic and would-be sympathetic, at the same time we awaken awareness among the apathetic. Already, among those who do care are many influencers in our society. But all of us can become influential on some level: We can influence others by talking and communicating via the Internet.

HEROES OF OUR USA EFFORT IN THEIR OWN WORDS

Customers Who Care

An American Dad

It is because of my two young children that I believe strongly in buying products made in the USA. Last Labor Day weekend, my wife and I took them camping. We enjoyed a campfire with a couple who help manufacture materials under contract for the U.S. Department of Defense. They had just been told that they may be out of work by January, due to outsourcing. Can you imagine?! Outsourcing work for our defense to foreign nations? And putting more Americans out of work in an ever-worsening economy? This is the not the future I want for my children—if it can even be said that they will have one!

S. Abrahamson
Massachusetts

A Concerned Mother

I received a call from our doctor's office about my son's test for lead in his blood. It was positive, but only 2.7. Nothing to worry about yet; not until it reached 10 would the doctor worry. However, I did a little research,

(continued)

(*continued*)

and it turns out that just a little bit of lead can cause many different problems, from growth to learning disabilities. The doctor gets worried only when the kidneys and liver start to shut down, which can happen at a 10 on the lead scale. They tried to tell me the lead was probably from the water, or even lead paint; but the water had been tested and our house had been painted properly, so no lead there. However, there had been a huge recall of a toy made in China, which had excess amounts of lead in it. My son, a typical four-year-old, put this toy in his mouth. Guess where he got the lead from? I proceeded to go through all of his toys and really looked at them; everything from China went out in the trash. I decided to buy him only USA-made toys from then on. I searched everywhere for them. My search started in 2006 on the Internet, when I could only find a few items. It is now 2010 and I have compiled a list that is seven pages long, in two columns. The list had grown with the many different items people have asked me to find, but, sadly, ebbed with those that have gone out of business.

In my search for these different items, I also realized that our economy is directly tied to the purchase of products made here. I was asked to give a talk on the importance of buying American at my local library; and from there the many different libraries in the area asked me to do the same. I complied, as I know the importance of doing so.

I recently found a matchbox-sized toy car line made in the USA. They are called Marble Racers, from Skullduggery. By buying them, here are the people I keep working: the manufacturer, the innovator, the draftsman, the craftsman, the packager, the truck driver that delivered them, the store that carries them, and the salesperson. I realize that there are many more people we keep working, but it is a circle of producer and buyer.

There comes a time when we all have to realize that if we don't purchase our own products, we will all ultimately be out of jobs. I am not an economist. I am not a politician. I'm just somebody who opened her eyes to what we are all doing to our own manufacturing base. I will continue to buy only USA-made items wherever I can find them, and to tell others why I do so. Someday, I hope we can bring this economy back up, but the only way we are going to do that is by purchasing from our own.

A Michigan Patriot

Straight Talk from the Granite State

I feel very strongly about buying American-made products and supporting businesses that manufacture goods here, for a variety of reasons. Probably the most important one is the ripple effect. When a consumer makes a decision to buy a product made overseas based only on cost (which is usually the case), that decision puts more and more people here, who would have manufactured that product, at risk of being laid off; or even cause a plant to shut down. When this happens, all of the small businesses around that factory are negatively affected, as well, whether it be a carpenter, truck driver, banker, realtor, shop owner. . . .

They are all at risk of losing their jobs, and the effect has tripled. Multiply this by at least 1,000 across the nation and we have a serious problem. No one seems to realize that a huge trade deficit also relates to a huge fiscal deficit. I do not believe this country has had a trade balance since the mid-1970s. When companies shut down and farm out their work overseas, along with them go all the tax revenues. And when Americans patronize foreign brands, those companies don't pay taxes here. It's all profit back to the mother country.

Second, if we reduce the manufacturing base to practically nothing, which is where we are headed, and ever had to wage large-scale war again, who would we be able to trust to manufacture our weapons, vehicles, planes, tanks, parts, and gear for the soldiers? China? Japan? Korea? Oh, they'll be glad to make them alright; but at what cost to us as a nation, and at what quality?

The lack of a true manufacturing base means the future of this country is very bleak. We cannot be a nation of service-only jobs, working as greeters at Wal-Mart or serving fast food at McDonald's, and support a healthy economy and earn a respectable wage. This creates a vast disparity between rich and poor; no in-between. I believe our own trade regulations have some decent protections in them, but they are not properly enforced, as everyone is afraid of "protectionism." Well, with record job losses and deficits, plant shutdowns, and high foreclosure rates, I think it is high time we have some protectionism to balance the trade deficit, so we can breathe again. Every other country does it; and some play unfairly, and yet we still trade with them. If we are not economically healthy, we cannot continue to help others around the globe; eventually, we will crumble from within.

G. Constantino
Real Estate Agent
Ossipee, New Hampshire

We must, as a group, overcome the complacency inspired by the siren songs sung on television and by politicians and marketers. We must help those among us who have thrown up their hands and come to believe lies like:

"It doesn't matter where it comes from."

"We live in a global economy."

"We're helping a third-world country to develop."

"There's no way to know what's really an American-made product these days, anyway."

We have to make them see that it does matter, that there is a solution, and that they can be a part of it. The key points we need to share are simple:

1. It is about our kids and the next generation; future jobs are declining and real wages are dropping.
2. Without real manufacturing, our economy will collapse.
3. Without a tax base, government at every level will suffer, and some will face bankruptcy.
4. American-made products are safer and of better quality; no American toy poisoned a kid in 2007.

The small percentage of us who actively care about this issue must take action to motivate the rest, starting with those who are sympathetic but haven't taken action yet, to think about these issues and do more themselves.

INFLUENCING PEOPLE

The nature of societal influence is changing. Trends are just as likely to take root and grow through the efforts of individuals, spreading from one person to the next and the next, through conversation, blogging, social media, activism, and other personal forms of action, as they are to begin in the mainstream media. Thanks to online outlets like blogs, Facebook, Twitter, and others, it's possible to influence thousands of people in a matter of minutes. They, in turn, can influence thousands of others; and the numbers continue to grow. I strongly encourage you to reach out to those around you in whatever way you feel most comfortable.

Each of us probably knows someone who really cares about buying American-made, but may not be aware of his or her options. Reaching out to those individuals is the first and easiest step on your journey, because these are the people who are aware of the problem and are most likely to act immediately when presented with solutions. They're also more likely to share what they've learned with like-minded others. But there is value in every conversation about this topic, regardless of the group the person you're chatting with falls into. Even if he or she may have little interest in helping, he or she probably knows someone who does, and may be willing to share the information.

When talking with others about this issue, I encourage you to ask who they know that cares the most about products made in the USA. You can be sure they know at least one person who feels strongly about it; and if they stop and think about it, they probably know several. The reply could be something like "Yeah, my Uncle Steve really does care; he has always been a real patriot. So does my friend Colleen, as her husband works in the union." Now such individuals begin to realize they can be helpful to the people in their lives by pointing out resources like MadeinUSAForever.com. At this point, their role shifts. They might not care about the larger issue, but almost certainly they'll be happy to pass along information that will benefit their friends and relatives who do care.

The goal is not just to get these people to listen to your opinion, but to visualize someone they know to whom they should mention it. This locks the idea into most folks' memories. You can be sure that the next time they see or talk to that individual, your conversation will pop back into active memory and be mentioned. This helps in three ways: First, the message makes its way to the individual who actively cares about buying USA-made products. Second, the person you originally told will bring it up with others when he or she realizes the message is relevant. His or her friend Melissa may not care so much, but her mother does, and so on. Third, that person who keeps mentioning it is very likely to eventually come around to buying American-made as well, as a direct result of engaging in conversation with multiple people who do see the value and respond eagerly to his information.

It is worth pointing out during these conversations the value of buying American-made, and where items are available, not just because it is helpful, valuable information to those that really care, but also because it helps to awaken the sleeping majority, who are mostly sympathetic to the cause, I believe. I often hear people complain that there are no American-made products available, simply because they are not immediately obvious on the shelves of the big retail chain stores where they shop regularly. Once they learn that there is at least an option available online, or that a particular local store does stock a higher than average number of American products, they realize they do have choices. Often, the retail chains do not want their consumers to know they have options, for the obvious reason that the stores are part of the import problem. Stirring our silent majority, and wakening them from their stupor on this issue, is key to getting the chain stores to start carrying American-made products, in the same way many grocery stores recently started offering organically grown foods.

We can throw a monkey wrench into the import plans of Wal-Mart and its ilk just by getting 5 to 10 percent of the American population actively looking for and buying American-made products. But to push this invasion of chintzy foreign products back into the sea, we must have the help of that now-silent but sympathetic majority on our nation's side. We cannot win this fight without their numbers; we must stand together as a nation if we are to make America whole again.

Though this group may not be aware of these issues before you chat with them, the basic beliefs are probably already in place. They just need concrete information about what is going on and how they can make a difference. Once you have stirred them to action, they will reach out to other sympathizers, in the millions.

Following this advice also solves the dilemma of what to get the person who wants only American-made products for the holidays. In 2007, during the Chinese lead poisoning crisis, when tens of millions of foreign toys were recalled, my wife and I were shocked that friends and relatives still gave our then-toddler daughter foreign-made toys. Headlines alerted us all to the dangers of these foreign imports, after lead was discovered in one toy after another, yet many buyers didn't change their buying patterns. You can be sure that we made most of those people aware enough of the issue that they did not repeat the mistake again in the years since, and can only hope that they extended the knowledge when making purchases for their own children, other friends, and relatives. We've received many, many calls at MadeinUSAForever.com from customers who bought something for a loved one who cares about this issue and made the recipient happy by being so considerate. We hear comments like, "Dad has always tried to buy American, but has had a hard time finding these products lately, so when we walked in with the shirt [or sweater, or other item], he was ecstatic and now wears it all the time." I can tell you from experience how heartening it is to be a part of that process, and to know that I'm helping people who truly care about rebuilding America to do their part and feel good about their choices. Anyone who chooses to share information about these problems and their solutions can be a part of that same process.

Trends in human behavior are not natural, like the seasons; they are created by people like you and me. Buyers at the big chain stores and foreign nations set this trade deficit trend in motion. Fashion magazines and designers may decide how tight jeans are going to be on starving models next year. Never forget, however, that it was individual consumers who launched the organic food movement that has been so successful at most food stores now. By being persistent, and ready to put their money where their mouths were, thousands of people influenced the corporate behavior of even some the country's largest grocery chains. Sure, it was helped along by some Hollywood types, and the media supported it, too, but long after the momentum of the consumer movement had reached critical mass. We can start such a trend by demanding that every chain store dedicates at least one section to only American-made items.

Until recently, we've been parties to this import trend, simply by not refusing to accept what the big chains serve up. However, as surely as this trend started, it can be reversed. Low, low prices without any concern about the cost to America, or to the workers, or to the environment? Enough! It's time to say no.

INFLUENCING RETAILERS

We are not the drones chain stores think we are, and any American company that treats us as such does not deserve our support or our business. It is only when we fail to act that we reward those businesses for treating us as if we're ignorant, lazy, and complacent; we teach them that they can continue to grow revenues by ignoring our real needs and failing to address the issues we care about. What else can we expect when we say, in effect, "I hate what you stand for. What you're doing is wrong. But here's my money anyway." The organic foods now available in many chain grocery stores are proof that we can influence the managers and owners of the giant companies if enough of us vote with our dollars, and make requests and voice complaints when they do not meet our needs. The independent stores or very small chains, where they still exist, are often bastions of American-made products, because they still remember what made this country great.

You'll find it is generally easy to make contact with a manager or other person who has authority in a store where you shop. You only have to ask. If he or she listens respectfully and follows up by taking action to buy American-made, give that store your wholehearted support. Admittedly, the bigger the chain the harder it will be to exert pressure, but it is still worth a try. Keep in mind, the local manager probably has very little say in which items are put on the shelves in the store, but he or she can pass on your comments to regional management. If enough people voice the same concerns, they will begin to reach the ears of the actual decision makers; and, eventually, the message will break through, in the same way the growing demand for organic food finally did.

You can also influence the big chains by writing a letter or sending an e-mail to their chief executive officers—and, if you're feeling really empowered, to their boards of directors, too. In general, you can find the names of these executives on company Web sites. I know for a fact from my years in the corporate world that any CEO's administrator will pay special attention to reasonably written notes from customers, and particularly from shareholders in that company. The last thing they want is to have to field embarrassing questions during a media interview or at a shareholder meeting; so if there is a trend, trust me, they will notice. Most CEOs probably won't actually read any of the letters, but if there are a hundred of them on the same topic, where last year there were two, they will be made aware of that. They always assume that one letter equates to hundreds or even thousands of concerned customers, since so few people bother to write.

Every day I give thanks to God for my family and their good health; then I give thanks because I get to spend each day and a good part of my nights being a part of the solution to the problems our nation faces. I know the odds are long, and realize this fight for our nation's future will be measured in terms of decades, not weeks, yet I am thankful. Thankful for the experiences I have had that helped me see the truth about free trade, and for having the gumption and ability to build the financial resources I would need to carry out this work. I'm also grateful I have the intellect to understand these complex problems, as well as the ethical beliefs that lead me to be troubled by them. And I hope to continue to develop the wisdom to do something meaningful about them.

I am also very grateful that so many good people are willing to take a stand alongside me. Without the thousands of you, my efforts at MadeinUSAForever.com would be for nothing. Every day thousands of you visit the Web site. Many share your thoughts and good wishes with us. This effort would be nowhere without you.

INFLUENCING WASHINGTON

Together, we can have more of an effect on Washington than many believe. Because the vast majority of citizens in this country are apathetic and never bother to contact their representatives, these men and women begin to take note when they start to hear from their constituents on a particular issue. And when they begin to receive a number of letters consistently expressing the same ideas or concerns, they recognize there is a lot of interest in the issue, even a movement afoot.

When I was in college, I got interested in a piece of legislation called the Taxpayers Bill of Rights, which was intended to limit the power of the IRS. My interest stemmed from watching a close friend of the family who was repeatedly audited. By contacting the staff aids to the members of the Senate and House committees on this legislation, I became friendly with several. One said to me, "Wow, eight people have called us about this issue today. What is going on?" I asked if that was considered a lot, and he told me they typically only heard from people about abortion rights. The point is, those eight calls were enough to make the staffer sit up and take notice.

Wal-Mart and the other big retailers, and even foreign manufacturers, are spending a lot of money to gain influence in Washington. This is distorting democracy, which is supposed to be "by the people and for the people." Presently, "we the people" are hardly even putting up a fight, so it is little wonder corporate entities have most of the influence on the trade issues in Washington.

We the people need to turn up the heat and make our senators and representatives personally responsible for how their votes affect American manufacturing. Let me clarify here: This does not mean helping an American company that makes its products abroad, as the Chamber of Commerce often does. As far as I am concerned, if a company does not produce its products here, it is not American at all. If an individual senator or representative is bowing to Wal-Mart, we need to make our voices heard in his or her home district. Every meeting with constituents should make that legislator wonder whether he or she is about to get nailed on for being in Wal-Mart's pocket, and for failing to address the foreign trade issue. It doesn't matter which party he or she is in, or what secret handshakes he or she may know. If that elected official is not looking out for America's interests first, we need to show him or her the door.

Wal-Mart, of course, has a lot more money to spend to sway Washington than we do—money that, ironically, comes from its customers who aren't speaking out. So we have work cut out for us. However, we also have what it takes; we have the power of the vote, the ultimate power. Frankly, Congress could use a lot more turnover anyway. Maybe it is in the fumes in the swamp Washington sits on, but these guys seem to become addicted to the façade of power. Lest they forget whose power it really is, we should show a lot more of them to the unemployment line.

I ask you to stand up and lock arms with me to take the fight to Washington, where we *can* change the priorities. There appear to be a few in each party who are sympathetic; now the rest need to be made to understand we are serious and determined. We can, peacefully (meaning *never* using violence) change the dynamic, if we are relentless. They will eventually do the right thing, even if it's only to get us off their backs.

They also need to be educated. Most are lawyers, but, ironically, law schools don't teach right from wrong. Law schools also do not teach history or world cultures. I have met hundreds of lawyers, some of whom were clearly smart people in their way; but their experiences and education had changed them. They were taught to find the "way out" for their clients, not necessarily to "do the right thing." The few

I met who had any international experience at all had typically spent six days at the nearest Hilton.

Our leadership desperately needs knowledge that goes well beyond an education in law. As I told you, I spent seven years living in Asia, and learned along the way the good and bad, the beautiful and ugly, of the cultures of those countries. For example, after I'd known him for many years, a good friend in Japan shared stories with me about his family's despair and suffering after World War II: the lack of food and the painful sacrifices that honed Japan into a nation that would rise like an economic phoenix in the 1960s and 1970s. Opening up like that is rare for the Japanese; they really have to know and trust you. Spending a few nights at the Shinjuku Hilton is hardly enough to even find out where to dine in the area, much less become an expert on the country.

If even a handful of legislators had actual experience in Asian business, our trade policies would be vastly different than they are today. They would be fair and balanced, and we would not be in this unsustainable situation we are today. Instead we have lawyers, many of whom go into politics because they hungry for power. They need to be motivated and educated, or shown the door. David Halberstam's *The Reckoning*, about the rise of Tokyo and Nissan and the issues with Washington and Detroit, is probably the best the book, among the hundreds I have read, at capturing the essence of the trade situation in the 1970s, when we started letting the tide turn against us.[1] It would be a good idea for our legislators to read this book, as it describes more than just our real place in the world; it makes it clear that there is a groundswell of folks who care.

Here's how you can take action. Both houses of Congress have Web sites, where it is easy to find out about your legislators and how to contact them. The House of Representatives Web site is www .House.gov; the Senate's is www.Senate.gov. In your e-mails, make sure to clearly state the issue and your stance on it in the first sentence, to ensure it gets to the right person on the politician's staff. This is critical, because senators and representatives rely on their staffers to understand the details and repercussions of the issues at hand.

We can, justifiably, complain about Washington all day long, but until we voice our concerns and state our position, in no uncertain terms, they will keep doing what they have always done. Take a stand with me. In addition to choosing to buy American and influencing our friends, we must hold Washington accountable. Washington reacts to pressure and stimulus. Stimulus primarily comes from cash, in amounts that the likes of Wal-Mart can spend to get what it wants; pressure comes from voter involvement and caring. We can do a lot more to counter big retailer money than many people realize, but it takes action. Let's take it!

PAY OUR OWN WAY

Let's face facts: We can talk the talk, but if we do not walk the walk, we are hypocrites. We need to check labels consistently, and we need to commit to buying American-made products.

Someone had to make everything we buy—not to mention the American suppliers that added parts for those products, and all the design, administration, and distribution work. The effect on these people and their livelihoods is very real. Every time we buy an item, we are either supporting our own economy or that of another country. That means we are either doing something positive for our own people or for foreigners. Someone had to make it. It is as simple as that. Then, in order for it to be profitable for that maker to continue putting it out there, someone has to buy it. It is as simple as that.

A small manufacturer called me recently and said, "Hey, we had to add two people because of you and MadeinUSAForever.com!" Those two people have hopes, dreams, and maybe a family to feed. The credit for those two new jobs doesn't really go to me, but to you, the people who buy those products. You can feel good about buying American-made products; it really does make a difference, and helps our people. A society is more than the sum of its parts. What each of us does and buys has a noticeable impact on those around us. Like it or not, understand it or not, we are *all* connected and intertwined. Our actions and purchases have a measurable effect on others, who in turn have an effect on us. By taking a little more time and/or spending a little more money, we can keep someone out of an unemployment line and give that man or woman the means and pride to build a better USA, who will, in turn, help us. You won't see the benefit on the price tag, but by keeping that person employed, your taxes will stay down because you will not have to pay for his or her welfare. It also means that individual is a lot less likely to cost your community by declaring bankruptcy or defaulting on the house down the street, and leaving it vacant, thereby lowering everybody's property values. To the contrary, rather than being a burden on society, that man or woman is helping it in the form of the taxes they pay and the purchases they make. Those benefits touch us all.

Here is what you can do: Check labels. Look for the "Made in USA" tag. Do a bit of research on the Internet before making purchases. Doing your part is actually a lot easier and more fun than you might think at first. Plus, you always get a good feeling when you do the right thing—the right thing for the person who made that item, the right thing for the American manufacturer, the right thing for your local economy and our nation, and the right thing for you, too!

I acknowledge, for some products it is very difficult to find American-made at reasonable prices, like toasters or watches. In these cases, what I recommend is to buy secondhand, by shopping on Web sites like Ebay.com. Here you can very often find old but never-used products that were set aside decades ago. They are often still in their original boxes! Better to recycle our money within our nation than to send it to foreign countries. I assure you that the quality of these American goods made years ago is much better than the chintzy foreign versions on shelves in stores today.

Keep in mind, we are all connected to one another economically in this nation, so whatever each of us can do to keep that money recycling here in the United States is better for us all. It is a proactive way of making ourselves and our nation stronger and healthier. That money you keep in our economy gives someone a job. That person can then put food on the table for his or her kids, provide for him- or herself, and make our communities a better place to live. That's how we can keep the virtuous economic circle turning.

Trickle-down economics, whereby the rich spending was supposed to rain pennies from heaven on the rest of us, gives us only one snapshot of a much bigger picture. The truth is, there is no trickle up or down. In a healthy economy, money does not flow one way or the other; it flows in all directions, recycling around and around in our nation—unless it is sent overseas when someone purchases an imported product.

MY CHOICE

I believe that I was put here for a purpose. I am not sure yet whether I went astray by climbing the corporate ladder and accumulating wealth while my country was growing poorer, or whether I was meant to learn a multitude of lessons from those experiences. What seems important to other people, the appearance of success and wealth, satisfied me for many years, too. What turned the tide for me was that I could not suppress my thirst for knowledge. That, for better or worse, kept my eyes open; and I could not suppress the knowledge I gained while in Asia, or what those realities meant for the future of our country. In addition, the lessons I learned and values I inherited growing up in the heartland kept me grounded. For example, I will never forget what I saw in Asia, past the glass towers: the kids on the streets without limbs, the mother feeding garbage to her toddler, the pollution spewing into the rivers and air. What we call "development" was not reaching them, because their own countries had other priorities. No one cares about these people, not even their own governments. Goals like overtaking the United States as the world's next superpower take priority. What a sad world it would be without the shining light of the USA touching and inspiring others around the globe. More than just examples of Asia's extremes, they are also examples of the extremes our own country will have to deal with if we do not avert the coming economic collapse. How long before little kids eating out of the garbage would become a common sight here? They may not be my children, but as a father I cannot tolerate the thought that such a childhood could one day become commonplace in this country. I had to do something, on so many levels.

I was an internationalist, flying between nations and earning a lot of money while my country grew weaker. The nation where I was raised, where I learned my values and faith, and where I was taught right from wrong, was starting to wane, even though I was personally thriving. The gifts I had been blessed with helped me become successful, but they also damned me by giving me the knowledge that the heartland was fading, and showing me that maybe I could do something about it. That awareness was like a heavy chain around my neck, one I managed to bear for some years. I even joked to a few friends that I could feel death's cold hand on my shoulder. In the end,

I decided to break that chain and do something. If our nation was a sinking ship, then I was going to go down with her, bailing to the last. I was determined to turn around and fight apathy and ignorance, alone if need be, to give my children the chance to experience our nation the way I had when I was a kid; a nation that had problems, yes, but where even the sky was no limit; a nation where real effort often led to reward; a nation where we never had to lock our houses or cars; a nation that was always striving to improve.

My choice was to quit that executive role to create MadeinUSA Forever.com. The change meant making a financial sacrifice, but it has been well worth it, to give Americans an easy and fun way to search the Internet for American-made products. Interestingly, from the moment the Web site went live, I became energized. Today, I am thankful for each visitor who comes, knowing that together we are doing something important for our suppliers and employees. Though I have never worked harder, I no longer feel burdened. Death and his cold hand have long since gone, too, replaced by the positive energy that flows by taking action to make a positive difference. Now that I have my purpose back I work seven days a week, yet it feels like a treat, not labor. I have not taken a penny in salary in the three years since the site launched, and I am thankful for that, too, because I have my soul back, paid for in hard labor. And I get to stand with those who also want to make a difference.

What if we fail? Taking that risk to do something worthwhile is well worth the effort and expense, many times over. Trying and failing, versus just catching the reruns on TV, makes for a life worth living. If it all collapses, at least on my deathbed (which I hope will be many years from now), I will be able to take solace in knowing I did my best for a just cause.

I bring not only my time and personal resources to this effort, but every lesson and trick I learned in Asia. I am playing for America, and I am playing to win. Sun Tzu said you must know your enemy to defeat your enemy. Fortunately, or perhaps unfortunately for them, I was a very good student.

Doing something meaningful for our nation does not feel like work at all to me. It is not a burden; compared to being a part of the problem, it is like carrying a feather.

Chapter 11 What Can Our Government Do?

Most days, it seems like our government is part of the problem instead of the solution. However, it is vital that government become part of the solution. Our government has the power and the ability to effect real and lasting change; all it lacks is the proper motivation. It's our job as citizens and voters to provide that motivation, to hold our elected officials accountable for the impact their actions (or inactions) have on our economy, on American companies, on Americans facing unemployment, on the environment, and on the quality of goods they allow into our country.

In light of the fact that we are confronting our greatest challenge since World War II, local, state, and federal governments need to form a different outlook. For the sake of our nation's economic future, we need a partnership among governments, businesses, and our people, all committed to private sector job creation. That can only be achieved through making products here in the USA. All parties must work together toward this goal—cards on the table, no hidden agendas.

LOCAL GOVERNMENTS

For a city or county to thrive, its citizens must have real jobs. By "real," I mean jobs that do not depend on city hall. Government-funded jobs are paid for by taxes, but in an era of declining industry, tax revenue is falling sharply, too, so there is no such thing as a "safe" local government budget, job, or pension anymore, as we slide further into economic decline. Attracting or growing manufacturing operations locally is the optimum choice for many communities, as only a very few tourist centers, like Orlando, Florida, can rely on the service industry to generate more than a small amount of tax revenue. Some people may think, "We get most of our tax revenues from property taxes on homes, so we are safe." That is a false hope if local industry is fading. Declining local economies put a lot of downward pressure on home values and reduce the number of new homes being built. If the underlying economic issues are not addressed, the reality will be a decaying tax base on homes, which could extend for decades or more. Even adding a casino, as Detroit did, cannot turn the tide. It is like putting a Band-Aid on a cancer patient.

Service-industry jobs within the community are important, yes, but they generally add value only when that community is healthy. Money to pay for those service jobs has to come from somewhere. For the vast majority of communities, that source can only be manufacturing. As I explained in previous chapters, manufacturing does more than create good jobs; it has a much more positive impact economically, due to the multiplier effect.

A mayor who is an effective leader knows and has a working relationship with every large business and a lot of smaller businesses in his or her community. On top of his or her list of concerns should be the health of every manufacturer, and what it would take get each of them to add 20 more jobs locally.

A lot of factories, even with the dire economic situation we face now, are running short of employees with certain technical skills. Once that pool of skilled workers gets depleted in an area, the management of a company will start to consider moving work to other facilities or even foreign countries. It is vital for the local leaders to, first, identify their communities' skill training needs; second, understand the deficiencies of the local workforce from the factories' perspective; and, third, work with the local school district and community colleges to make sure that these skills are being taught. In my 20 years in business, the only time I was personally aware of being sought out by the local government, beyond getting tax bills, is when I was being solicited for donations.

HEROES OF OUR USA EFFORT IN THEIR OWN WORDS

Crafting Excellence One Pair at a Time: Footskins

We at Footskins feel strongly about supporting the United States, the country our founding fathers established based on strong principles of liberty, which include the free market system. Footwear by Footskins began with skills passed down from an American craftsman who had handcrafted leather footwear for decades. We continue that tradition, and will always remain in the USA.

We are a small family-type business with all American workers, so it's our livelihood—we will never outsource abroad. Being in the United States, we also use American leathers and many other U.S. components. We are finding an ever-increasing demand for American-made footwear and other products.

We operate our business according to the principles of honesty and integrity; and the workers here at Footskins live by the golden rule to treat others as they want to be treated. Each worker takes personal responsibility for producing quality products. The resulting quality and workmanship are what people have come to depend on from us, pair after pair.

With so many companies going overseas, we fear the United States is losing the capabilities, skills, and machinery to even be able to manufacture products (including shoes) in our own country, making us more and more dependent on foreign countries. Fewer American manufacturers mean fewer available materials and at costs higher for those who remain here. There certainly is more accountability for manufacturing here in the States, resulting in higher-quality and safer products. In addition, as technology and communications continue to spread around the world, cheap labor in other countries will very likely become less available as workers become less willing to work for low wages.

(continued)

(*continued*)

We at Footwear by Footskins believe in the free market system, where the best products endure and prosper. America needs to return to a producer-based economy, which raises the standard of living, rather than continue as a consumer-based economy. It is such founding principles that have made America great; as a result, this country has always had a higher standard of living than anywhere else in the world. We believe it has been put by God into our nature, as a nation, to improve ourselves and be free.

Local government administrators and planners are starting to understand that manufacturing jobs add a lot more value to their economies than service jobs. The large amount of taxes that factories and their employees pay into local and state coffers are more than just a boon; they make it possible for a modern economy to appropriately fund local government activities. The highly skilled employees at these facilities are paid a premium, and that premium recycles into every part of that community, from the products individuals and families buy to the taxes they pay.

City governments need to fully understand the skills that local private employers are searching for, especially where deficiencies in particular labor skills might be hindering those facilities. For example, if discussions with local manufacturers reveal that they are concerned because they are unable to locate enough employees within the community who have a specific tooling skill, by addressing that training need among the unemployed, government officials will accomplish two important goals: They will prevent that company from shifting work elsewhere, and be able to move some people from the unemployment lines into good-paying jobs!

The health of a community depends on two factors: the unemployment rate and local wages. Families that earn more generally spend more in their community, thereby helping to energize that community. Therefore, local government has to recognize what it takes to get its employers to add jobs, and then to attract the jobs with better wages to the community.

This partnership between local business and government should be focused on protecting and growing the community. In this relationship, all parties involved are partners; no one has a license to line its pockets or bend laws of any sort. This has to be a real partnership, an alliance, between equals. Cards need to be on the table for every issue under discussion. If, for example, the city spends money to add an educational program, because the business partner said it was necessary in order to expand, the business must meet its commitment to hire locally. Similarly, the city must keep up its end of the agreement by, for example, arranging adult training programs to improve the skills of potential employees.

In most situations, it is much easier to convince existing local businesses and factories to expand local production than it is to attract a brand-new facility. I often read about a state that has spent tens of millions of dollars to attract a foreign factory, when a small fraction of that might have kept an existing facility operating in that community. Understanding existing assets (factories) and helping them survive and expand translates directly into local jobs. It must be a priority of all government leaders, no matter what their party politics. We are all in this together.

Not surprisingly, businesses really do value government relationships when they spend thousands or even millions on local facilities. Executives at my former employer often talked up their local government relationships—which were not, unfortunately in the United States, but in Malaysia and Thailand. In Malaysia, where Western Digital's production makes up a considerable amount of the GNP, the company has a special relationship with the government. It goes without saying that it receives tax breaks and benefits from employee training programs; but the relationship runs much deeper than that. I remember sitting with the then-CEO in a meeting in Tokyo. He had just flown in from Malaysia, where an uprising was then underway. He told us that the government had assured him that, if need be, they would surround the company's production facilities with tanks to make sure they could keep producing. Thankfully, it did not come to that. At the time, the hourly wage in Malaysia was many times that of rural China; but with that kind of open connection and solid relationship with the local government, to this day Western Digital makes tens of millions of hard drives there annually.

Communities do not have to throw around millions of dollars to be appealing to companies. For example, making sure local vacant facilities are in usable condition, and offering them at very nominal rents, might be one way to attract a new manufacturing facility without spending much taxpayer revenue during these troubled times.

Local tax incentives also could be better spent. For example, tax incentives in many communities are often used to build strip malls rather than to renew downtown areas. These malls take business away from the traditional heart of the city. This money would be much better spent by protecting businesses that are already there and by making the community a place where a business would want to build a new facility or take over an old one. Spending hundreds of millions on a new football or baseball stadium while the roads crumble is not only a poor spending choice, it fails to attract viable manufacturers.

What makes a community appealing to a businessperson who is "shopping" locations? Based on my conversations with several of MadeinUSAForever.com's hundreds of suppliers, coupled with my years of experience in big business, this is what I learned:

1. *Good schools*: The local educational system is important, for two reasons: One, the company wants to know that it can count on a steady supply of qualified workers; and, two, most of the company's managers will be sending their children to local schools.

2. *Safety*: Management wants to be sure not only that their facilities are safe, but that their families are safe in their homes and on the streets. No managers will push for a plant to be built in a community where they will be afraid to let their children go outside to play. If the most basic level of safety in a community is not met, it's an indication of dangerous social problems in the community, and makes it very hard to attract valuable business, without paying a fortune that the community probably does not have.

3. *Availability of skilled labor*: This goes hand in hand with the schools requirement, but is so important it deserves to be reiterated. And notice that this is higher on the list than either wages or taxes. A plant that cannot adequately staff its operations with skilled workers will look elsewhere for those employees.

4. *Tax levels*: Taxes need to be balanced between level of services and the payout. The business could move out to the desert, for example, and incur almost no taxes; but that does not happen. Nor does a business want to move to a community or state where taxes are too high relative to the services. This applies to both

business taxes and individual income taxes. In theory, executives might consider a location based only on corporate taxes, to gauge what is best for the company; but in reality, they are very concerned about that personal income tax, too.

5. *Quality of wages and employees*: Wages must be fair, based on the level of skills required. Businesses are concerned about more than just cheap wages; they know they need employees who are hardworking and skilled. And if management is wise, they also want employees with gumption. The best employees usually are not the cheapest, nor the easiest to manage.

6. *Good standard of living*: Managers do not want to live in the middle of nowhere, with nothing for them or their families to do. A high quality of life in a given community is a much stronger draw for a business than can be justified on paper. From camping to good restaurants, quality of life includes anything that could make the community an appealing place to live and work.

7. *State/local leadership*: The more problematic the governor (sorry California, New York, and, especially, Illinois), the more difficult it is for businesses to take seriously the prospect of investing in the community. Are local government leaders partners, or big parts of the problem? Local leaders who are willing to work as a team in a productive way with businesses are huge assets to their communities. Those who are constantly embroiled in conflicts, personal or political, are likely to scare away billions of dollars of potential investment.

8. *Financial stability*: The assurance that a community is not in danger of bankruptcy or cutbacks in basic services, just to pay for bloated pensions of former city managers, is an important incentive for businesses. Conversely, before agreeing to any deals or concessions, government at all levels should vet the financial condition of prospective businesses to their communities. Either party being dishonest about the state of its finances is sure to spoil what could otherwise be a productive, multiyear alliance.

9. *The whole package*: Is there one compelling factor or set of factors that brings it all together? Is there one deal maker or breaker? California, though it has a lot to offer, is hampered by high taxes and questionable government stability. Nevada has very low taxes, but lacks skilled machinists and such. Michigan has a stable workforce and a high quality of life; but it needs to address state government and tax issues before it can be truly attractive

to business. Every state and community has its story, and the smart businessperson will be looking at every facet of it to determine what the overall experience of operating a facility in a community will truly be like.

Local government officials need to network with a broad spectrum of business leaders, and be able to sell them on the reasons their community is the place to put a new facility. At the same time, local businesses already in place should not be overlooked; they should be able to trust that local government will be fair and responsive to their needs, too.

Few in a community know it as well as its local government leaders. When they work with citizens and local businesses to address weaknesses and enhance strengths, it energizes the community and goes a long way toward accomplishing its goals. As thousands of communities, their local governments, and businesses become active partners in this way, our nation will be firmly on the path to renewal.

Rebuilding the USA depends on thousands of communities and local governments becoming strong links in the renewal chain, and committing to going the extra mile. Now is the time for local leaders to step up, as they did in the days when these communities were founded. When local governments stand up for our economy and American manufacturing, our effort to turn this situation around will be strengthened manyfold. Join the movement. Be a local hero!

THE STATE LEVEL

State-level government is also crucial to America's renewal. Just as a city's mayor should be very familiar with the businesses that make his or her community tick, governors and their staffs should put themselves on the front line to protect manufacturing jobs statewide; more, they should become deeply involved in wooing businesses and factories back from China and other low-wage nations.

With a thorough understanding of what attracts, and detracts, potential investors, state government can be instrumental in making their communities better places to build or expand a factory. With respect to our current dire economic situation and the vital efforts going on to repair it, every decision needs to be considered within the context of its impact on local economies. Before making any decision, ask whether it would, for example, add a burden on Illinois businesses that those in Indiana and other nearby states do not have? Would it make manufacturers more or less likely to invest in the state? Would it increase or decrease perceived stability? How would it affect private sector employment and wages? To answer these questions, it's essential to be able to have an honest, open relationship with businesspeople who have decision-making power. (Note: Very often in these situations these people are a lot lower on the corporate ladder than CEOs.)

The ideal governor would be both a realist and cheerleader, a politician who understands his or her state's strengths and weaknesses intimately, and is capable of leading the charge for renewal and in seeking new investment. Growing an economy is like growing a garden. Some flowers bloom early in the season, but don't last beyond the first frost. Other hardier plants and trees take many years of nurturing before they mature, but they can last for generations. A good governor is like a master gardener and caretaker, someone who watches over and helps the economy to grow.

The days of laissez-faire state governments—leaving growth to the market and hoping industries will be attracted to their states—are long over. If one state is not out meeting with businesspeople and agreeing on reasonable requirements, the next state over will be. And that's the state that will attract those factories and jobs. I am not recommending that states engage in ridiculous bidding wars with other states to get a plant built. Promising tens of millions or more in assistance to win business is counterproductive. That is far different from recognizing that infrastructure like roads and sewers need to meet certain minimum requirements. A balance has to be maintained; a state has to weigh the money it would have to invest in order to lock down an agreement on a new manufacturing facility against the benefits that facility would bring to the state.

It's also important that state governments coordinate to some degree with a more proactive federal government, in order to better protect and expand on existing manufacturing facilities; to maximize the construction of new facilities; and to effectively upgrade and market former government and military facilities that already have some infrastructure.

Some states might consider waiving their local sales tax for products made within their borders, to some threshold of value added for 5 or 10 years, until industry can be rebuilt. Such incentives are not the same as corporate handouts; they are offered to nurture and encourage investments in the state's economy.

I grew up in Illinois, though I currently live California because I work in the high-tech industry. Both are gridlocked, upstate versus downstate, suburb versus city, and virtually any other way a state can split. (I sure can pick 'em!)

For the sake of our nation, it is time for every state to stop the internal bickering and politicking for the next few years and do what is necessary to rebuild the USA. State governments looking proactively for ways to make local manufacturing more of a benefit and less of a burden for business would help us emerge from this economic downturn. They can and should be the engines of future growth.

THE FEDERAL LEVEL

Our federal government could play the leading role in rebuilding our nation if it could just put aside business as usual and make stewardship of our nation its primary goal.

First and foremost, the federal government—regardless of party or bureaucratic entity—has to recognize the vital importance of manufacturing to our economy, as other successful nations do. We can no longer rest on our laurels; it is not 1960 anymore. For all intents and purposes, we gave away our superpower status when we allowed our factories to be shipped abroad. With them, we gave away good jobs and our future ability to sustain our national security. It does not have to be that way. We can still turn it around and rebuild this country on our own terms, if the federal government is willing to act. Like state and local governments, the federal government must consider every decision it makes in terms of advancing our country's manufacturing base.

The federal government needs to put emergency plans into operation, immediately, to deal with both the goods and energy trade deficits. Instead of spending hundreds of billions in places like Iraq, we need to invest in the effort to break the shackles of both these deficits, so that we can turn around this great nation.

Will it be hard work? Absolutely. Might we fail? Success is far from guaranteed. However, I truly believe that once we gain momentum as a nation, we will accomplish great things, much as we did during World War II. One thing is certain: If we fail to act, we will fail.

Any politician or government official who thinks it is a good idea to close plants and move them abroad should leave his or her government job and go to live in those countries. Both parties have to come together on this issue, and stop the daily nonsense of petty attacks in the media. We are in an economic crisis of historic magnitude. If there is to be a political competition, let it be over which party can benefit the country most by rebuilding our manufacturing base and putting an end to both the trade and energy deficits. By attacking these issues head-on now we will have a fighting chance to avert a Great Depression-like collapse in the future. Let us make the hard choices now, while we still can.

For the next five years, every decision and every policy should be geared to maximizing manufacturing jobs and eliminating our dependence on foreign goods and energy. Those trillions of dollars now hemorrhaging from our nation's coffers will then be recycled back into our economy, renewing our nation and giving good-paying jobs to millions of unemployed, jobs they can take pride in.

Let us not judge our current government leaders by the mistakes of others. Let's judge them based on tangible, immediate efforts and near- and long-term results. In the end, we will all be history, which is always the much harsher judge. Better to be remembered in the history books as going down fighting than for being skilled at dodging or responding to daily media attacks. Effective government leadership will be remembered for its efforts, just as a lack of that leadership will be remembered as craven. As long as I can hold out physically, I will be in the trenches fighting, alongside those of you who care about our nation. And I intend to make sure that our struggle is well documented for history, both the heroic and craven efforts of individuals in the federal government.

To start its effort, the federal government could convene a nationwide 90-day Internet and live town hall brainstorming session where every citizen from every walk of life could contribute ideas for turning this situation around. Such an event would generate concepts and possible solutions at a magnitude rarely seen in history.

Do you feel the energy already?

The cool thing about brainstorming is that no idea is a bad idea. All voices are welcomed and respected. The more valuable, workable ideas will float to the top naturally, where they can be nurtured by our leadership while they prepare policies to be implemented as soon as possible after the 90-day session.

Here are a few brainstorming ideas to get you thinking:

- Waive sales taxes nationwide for products that qualify as "Made in USA" for five years or more. That would encourage domestic production without having to use tariffs against foreign makers. Foreigners don't like it? Too bad.

- Allow investment in production equipment for use within the USA to fully depreciate within a year, if the business chooses, and a tax credit. The tax credit would be repaid, plus 50 percent, if the equipment was not used in the United States within a year or was shipped or sold to another country.

- Broaden the list of items considered important for national security and put them under protection from imports for the next decade, or longer. (This is very common in nations like Japan and China.)

- Encourage foreign companies to partner with American companies to build production facilities for items that we no longer make here. For example, it is tragic that of the tens of millions of liquid crystal displays (LCD) and plasma televisions sold here today, none of the displays are made in the USA. A few companies screw on the frame and market it as assembled here; but sorry Vizio, we know you are not adding real value. For LCD and plasma televisions, the value is the display itself. We could encourage a company like Sharp or Panasonic to partner with an American company like GE (assuming it chooses to be American again), HP, or even Intel, and add special tax benefits. The Japanese or Taiwanese firms would see the wisdom of this, if they were sure we were serious from a long-term perspective. For example, the Japanese company Sharp, which produces LCDs for use in televisions, has the critical expertise and knowledge of production techniques to get around Japan's relatively high wage rates. The American partner would bring local marketing expertise and engineering skills to the table—and, yes, the deal would guarantee perpetual access to our market. It sure would be great to have a television that was actually made here again.

These are just a few ideas. What would you suggest?

On so many levels, our federal government holds the keys, making our success is this effort dependent on its participation. We have to urge legislators to stop bickering and come together to do the right things for our nation.

The "right things" mean in-depth discussions followed by definitive action. For example, to deal with the energy deficit, find out what would be the costs, time frames, and savings associated with upgrading our nation's power plants at the expense of a shared utility tax. If we are going to make changes in time to see material results, the most important step is to move beyond talk and into action.

Time is short, and we need effective leadership from governments at every level. Not since World War II have we faced a situation so serious. Rather than politicians who lust for power, we need men and women who want to serve because it is the right thing to do; not for any sort of personal gain, and fully aware there is an emotional and physical cost to being part of the solution in government. We need our best and brightest to do what many probably dread: become involved with our government at every level, and be a part of the solution.

Chapter 12 What Should Companies Do?

I know from my decades as a corporate ladder climber that business is both a major cause of America's economic decline and a crucial link to its recovery. Some businesses sold out our great nation to save a few pennies; then, instead of reinvesting in America, they bled America dry while paying their CEOs fortunes beyond what any individual is worth. Still, business can be, indeed must be, a big part of the solution. Business must break through the false perception that the United States is no longer a manufacturing nation. Business must invest here, must nurture and train a new generation, to give them hope and a stake in our unique culture and nation. American businesses must take a stand; they must power the engine that awakens this phoenix and enables her to fly.

As I have discussed, I observed firsthand that Japanese companies put their own first, as do Korean companies, and others. Our companies used to operate under this philosophy, too, and it is time for

American companies to do so again. This is more important than whether a corporation earns a penny more per share than expectations; this about our survival as a people and a nation.

It can be done.

If a company is based here and expects our government to provide assistance in its time of need, then it has to put American citizens first. For example, if GE and Whirlpool both fell on hard times and asked for government assistance, before doling it out, the government should first review them for the damage they have done by moving plants abroad. GE has led the charge in moving manufacturing abroad, whereas Whirlpool has kept a lot production here. Clearly, in a time of great need, the one that has been more committed to the USA should receive assistance, while the one that has caused so much destruction to our economy should be allowed to collapse.

This is not to say that American companies supporting Americans first should be just an insurance policy. Adhering to this business philosophy is in their best interest, in that they are supporting their own key customer base. Killing off good jobs here is not only wrong, it is shortsighted. Those same employees buy products from them and other American companies.

I realize it is difficult for a corporation to think beyond the short-term savings of a few cents; but in the long term, it's their own business, as well as that of other American companies, that will suffer. When retailers like Wal-Mart force a domestic plant to close because they import more products from China, they are putting their own customers out on the street. Multiply that by thousands of plants and millions of workers. To pretend our largest retailer is not having a direct negative effect on millions in both groups is to be either naïve or willfully ignorant. Yes, there may be short-term costs associated with prioritizing America and its future, but the long-term payoff will benefit all of us, including the businesses making that investment. Businesses in other countries have long managed to remain profitable while maintaining loyalty to their homelands.

Our own corporations have opened the floodgates to chintzy foreign goods, but the smart ones of the next generation will be those that recognize the value of producing here—not to mention an asset called loyalty. Many of our manufacturers moved production abroad yet left their label on their products. Later, they even gave up on that and contracted out manufacturing to nations that hate us. Our big retail chains used their massive bulk purchasing to further undermine our economy. Plus, they pay their employees too little. According to the Bureau of Labor Statistics, the median income of a sales clerk at a big retailer is barely over $20,000, about 40 percent less than the national average.[1]

Smart companies recognize the value of making their products here. China's cost advantages will eventually start to disappear, particularly when Washington finally gets the courage to force them to stop manipulating its currency beyond the usual few percent its government allows its currency to float. When that happens, companies here in the United States that maintained and nurtured their American workforces will earn a huge dividend, in that they will be able to take advantage of future growth, while those that shuttered their factories will be left to fend for themselves.

Supporting our nation first is not only the patriotic and right thing to do for our nation, but it is actually smart business. Here is why:

CUSTOMER BASIS

There is a growing movement of Americans from every walk of life who care about American manufacturing and are making it a higher priority when making purchases. Already, smart companies are ready and willing to service this expanding base of customers, not necessarily because they care about the issue but simply because being responsive to customer demands improves their own bottom lines.

Often, commitment to purchasing American-made components and manufacturing goods in America goes hand in hand with a commitment to quality, commitments rarely made by those manufacturers that place cost savings above all else. For example, in the sports clothing arena, unlike Nike and Under Armor, which make almost nothing in the USA, Wickers has made the commitment to produce 100 percent American-made exercise wear. Wickers' products costs a bit more, yes, but the company sells only the highest-quality goods, with the expectation that its customers will use them for many years. I can assure you, it's the real deal. I wear Wickers' products nearly every day. I bought some for use at the gym and found it so comfortable I was soon wearing it even to meetings in places like Hong Kong,

Beijing, Kuala Lampur, and Singapore, where the heat and humidity were unbearable. I had tried many alternatives to protect against the burning heat and intense humidity, but none compared to Wickers. I sat in a suit and tie with my Wickers underwear on, comfortable while even the locals dripped sweat. That is an edge I never had wearing any of the Nike or Under Armor clothing I ever bought. That's American quality: It measures up and is truly focused on the customer.

Unfortunately, as I've noted previously, with so many so-called American companies producing their goods overseas, it's not always immediately clear which products are American-made and which are not. Everyone in the business world knows that these chintzy imports are little more than planned obsolescence at work; they expect items to wear out quickly, forcing people to buy replacements sooner. Big retail chains price low, but with quality to match, the point being to draw customers back soon to replace those items. These chains also claim to offer value, all the while hoping that customers won't do the math and realize that they're not really saving money over time. This scam has worked well for Wal-Mart and other large retailers for a long time, but the jig is up. More and more customers are realizing that this is just a shell game to get more money out of them. This game has been so lucrative for the big retail chains that it will be difficult for them to shift gears and offer true value. Some may not be able to do it at all, and will fade into history. Value—by which I mean excellent quality combined with a fair price, rather than a cheap up-front price for trash—is the new rule of the day, and will be the rule for decades to come.

The American suppliers that I know well never gave up on this model of excellence at a fair price. They've always been conscious of the fact that a $35 pair of American-made jeans that lasts for five years is a better deal than a $20 pair of jeans from China that lasts for a year. The American pair has a higher up-front cost, but is much cheaper in the long run, because replacing the Chinese-made pair means spending $100 over five years, versus $35 over five years for the American-made jeans. Unfortunately, many consumers don't look beyond the initial price. They've been conditioned by large retail chains to focus on short-term savings and compare only what they see on the price tags.

Just as it's clear that a customer is saving more by spending $35 over five years than $100 over five years, it's also apparent that these retailers would prefer receiving $100 over $35. But customers are figuring this out, too; they are starting to do the math. They know it is better for the environment to buy one good product that lasts than five that will end up in the landfill sooner. They also are becoming more aware of working conditions abroad that allow production at such low prices, and are beginning to grasp the value of having American workers once again producing high-quality goods for us.

Sorry Wal-Mart, but your game is nearing its end. Within the next three to five years, those manufacturers and retailers that join the value trend and make their products here will hit a homerun with customers. Fortunately, the right thing to do for our country is also a sound business decision.

Charging a higher price for much better-quality items that last a lot longer is the wave of the future; coincidentally, it was the way of our past, as well. Our grandparents didn't have homes full of cheaply made items that had to be replaced frequently. They had the same television for 15 years, slept their whole married lives in the bed they were given as a wedding gift, and served dinner to their children and grandchildren on the same dining room table they bought as newlyweds. As I write this sentence I am sitting next to some of my grandparents' furniture from the fifties; its solid quality puts any furniture from China to shame. Lasting value we can count on is the American way.

To date, traditional retail chains have been slow to become part of the solution, whereas Internet-based retailers have been leading the way in breaking barriers and giving folks real choices again. Maybe the big retail chain store down the street won't give you an American-made, high-quality, high-value choice, but that doesn't mean you don't have options. You can find help at MadeinUSAForever.com, 24 hours a day 7 days a week, year-round. Eighty percent of our shipments are on their way within two business days. We care about repeat customers. Every order that leaves our warehouse includes a thank-you note, signed by me personally. We will always seek to extend the boundaries of excellence, in our ongoing effort to offer only high-quality American-made products and the best customer care, with a real personal touch. That is what I believe in.

As customers again come to recognize the value of buying American-made products, those companies that manufacture here, or sell products manufactured here, will gain their long-term loyalty, as well as the advantage over their competitors.

WORKER ADVANTAGE

As a former corporate finance executive who was personally familiar with the real cost numbers, I want to stress this point: Now is not the time to give up on American workers, either from a cost perspective or with regard to our nation's future. The advantages of having a ready, highly motivated American workforce in place will make the difference for smart companies and our nation's future in the coming years. It is time for every company that considers itself American to make sure it has the workers it needs in place.

Let me prove to you that wages comprise only a small part of the cost difference. "Mass production" means, literally, making tens of millions of units of many of the items being produced. The dollar amount is spread across so many units that the actual wage difference becomes nominal. The more units produced per hour per employee, the less noticeable the wage difference, even compared with other variable costs, like materials or scrap rate. It is second nature to American workers to keep these other costs down.

Let's call a spade a spade: The true cost advantage in China stems from other factors, among them currency manipulation, lack of environmental controls, and poor worker safety, as I've explained earlier. Moral and long-term economic concerns aside, those advantages will disappear over time, one way or another. To the extent that the wage difference is a factor, it is really just a matter of exchange rate differences. For example, when the yen-to-dollar exchange rate was about 200 yen per dollar a few decades ago, Japan had a labor cost advantage; today, the yen-to-dollar exchange rate is 80 yen per dollar, and the labor cost situation has flipped. Currently, Japan is far from being a cheap place to manufacture, from a labor perspective. Once China's artificial hold over its currency breaks, its wage levels will surge, in terms of dollars.

PRIDE IN WORKMANSHIP

My former corporate colleagues who take the easy route to saving money today miss the big picture. With rare exceptions in this country, we do the right thing with regard to employee safety and the environment; in other nations, they simply do not. However, foreign workers will not tolerate such conditions forever, much less the cancer-causing agents spewing into the air they breathe and the water they drink.

Instead of closing factories, we should challenge companies across the board to do more with less, to innovate to overcome China's cost advantage. No one knows how to build products better than the American worker, who builds it every day.

There are always individual exceptions, but the average American worker is very hard-working and conscientious. Japanese excel at repetitive-motion manufacturing, but just try to get them to stand up and say, "No, this is wrong. We can do this process better through XXX." That is the value of the American worker, and though it may be a bit harder to manage employees who are more likely to question processes, such individuals bring about innovation. I have seen factories all over Asia, but I have never seen one that has better workers than our people. The argument has never been about whether American workers are capable; it has been about the savings that can be garnered through exploitation in the third world.

It makes sense for U.S. businesses to ensure a future American workforce by nurturing and educating our people to build their products now and in the future. Those companies that have given up on the American worker will be left out in the cold when the tide turns, for whatever reason, and manufacturing comes back to the USA.

TIMELINESS

Change is coming. The trade imbalance cannot last forever. If this country doesn't act to fix the problem, either China will cease to maintain its artificially low cost advantage, or an economic collapse here, sparked by Washington's debt going into default, will undermine the value of the dollar. One of these alternatives will shift the dynamics of the trade issue. Regardless of how the change comes about, the advantage for years to come will go to those companies that already manufacture here. Those firms that stopped production in the USA have a choice to make: Either they move their manufacturing back to this country now, on their terms, or face a much more dire future. Those manufacturers wise enough to invest in the USA before it becomes obvious that they have no choice will be poised to survive future economic storms. Those that depend solely or almost exclusively on foreign manufacturers will not be in a position to deal with the coming changes, financially or operationally. Simply put, they will not get the product they need to sell at anywhere near the price they want.

From a timeliness standpoint, an organization's ability to survive and prosper, no matter what the economy brings, will depend on having the equipment and skilled American workforce to produce, while other companies flounder. These facilities cannot be built overnight; neither can workers be trained overnight. Once management decides to build a factory, it may take three to five years before it is fully operational. That's long enough to put a company out of business if it has moved its production to Chinese contractors but can no longer get product at the low rates it anticipated. The same is true for the retail chains. Today, they count only the cost advantage of buying as much from China as possible; that will not be the case forever. The tide will turn. That change may seem sudden to the unprepared, but it's already becoming obvious that this artificial trade situation cannot continue forever.

What happens when those chintzy imports are no longer available at anywhere near today's prices? Big retail chains no longer have the relationships in place here in the United States to fill their shelves. Some, like Wal-Mart, have burned so many bridges among American manufacturers that their options may be severely limited. Even if they are able to buy American, they will not be able to do so at anywhere near the wholesale prices they have forced down vendors' throats in the past. The way that Wal-Mart and some other large retailers have been treating their suppliers, and even their own workers, is already common knowledge among the general public, and their bad reputation will be hard to shake.

Chain stores that form solid relationships with American manufacturers early will be rewarded in several ways. First, no matter what may be going on in the outside world, with factories and mills here in the United States only a short train or truck ride away from those retailers, they will still be able to stock their shelves. Second, they will be able to promote early and often their commitment to buying

American-made, thus showing support for their customer's jobs and wage levels. Already, these customers number in the millions and are very loyal to those they know have a strong commitment to the United States. Third, costs will shift, prices will move back into balance, and the benefits will go to those working with American manufacturers. The retail chains with the foresight to build long-term buying relationships with American manufacturers will find they are getting better wholesale costs than those retail chains like Wal-Mart that tried to put a bullet in the head of American manufacturing.

The American customer and manufacturer will remember which retailers were with them and which were against them, when the time comes. Supporting American manufacturing is not just an opportunity to weather, and even profit in, any storm; it is, in fact, the ultimate insurance policy.

OUR PURPOSE

Companies from other countries that sell here view their purpose as supporting the fabric of their homelands. Knowing that, doesn't it make sense that our companies should do the same?

Are we Americans in business just to squeeze that last penny out of the customer, so that CEOs can go on another binge? No. We Americans are a part of something greater, and our companies need to step up and be stewards in the communities where they operate.

Do you want to be just another businessperson who got by today by selling out America's future, with the knowledge that your children and grandchildren will be facing sharply lower living standards, and that they will be aware you could have done something about it, but chose not to? All American businesspeople need to consider our nation's future and decide whose side they are on. Will they be part of the solution, and bring good manufacturing jobs back to the USA? Or will they choose to continue to outsource our great nation, into oblivion? The time is past for burying our heads in the sand and pretending that it is none of our concern. As American businessmen and women, we are either part of the solution or part of the problem. No more hiding. It is time to take sides.

We are Americans, and inescapably a part of the future of our nation. Whether it decays or reaches new heights of greatness, we will share its common destiny—one also shared with our children, grandchildren, and beyond. It is time to do right by the USA in each and every decision we make. Shareholders with a stake in these companies need to make sure management is accountable. But whether we own a thousand shares of stock or none at all, we are all stakeholders in these companies, for they affect the future of our nation.

The first thing a CEO should mention when he or she stands before shareholders is how the company helped this country profit, and made it better place, this week, month, quarter, and year. Along with the discussion on profits and revenue, the CEO should detail what he or she did for our nation. The goal of rebuilding American manufacturing and the economy should not be in conflict with the long-term profitability of the company. The two go hand in hand. Customers will sense the difference, and reward businesses that are doing their best for America, versus those that are hurting America. Smart, concerned customers will stop patronizing those that continue to sell out this country.

Our purpose as American businessmen and women is to build our companies in ways that complement and enhance our great nation, not harm it to save a few pennies. This doesn't mean that American business should do Washington's bidding—as everyone knows, our government has many problems of its own to solve. It is usually not all that difficult to see where America's, and thus, typically, our own, interests lie in a given situation. For example, I became involved in heated arguments at a former company over whether patents developed in California should be transferred to an Asian subsidiary, in order to artificially lower the firm's tax liability in the United States. Though the patents had been developed using tax credits from the State of California, there were legal loopholes that could conceivably have allowed their transfer to Asia. That would allow the mother company to pay lower taxes overall by, in effect, artificially setting a lease rate to charge it for its own patents. This sort of internationalist sleight of hand is disgraceful, and is only possible when the accountants most devoid of ethics also have law degrees. California, already hemorrhaging cash, had come up with a plan to subsidize research and development, in a desperate attempt to keep the fires of innovation burning there. Unfortunately, government did not anticipate antics like this. When consultants start openly equating legal and ethical practices, you know there is going to be trouble. I left before the matter was settled, but hope for the best for this company, which generally operated very ethically.

When we make decisions to improve our companies from an American perspective, we make our communities better, too. Enough of those improvements add up to strengthen our nation overall. The positive economic effect eventually puts more money into the hands of our customers. Therefore, doing the right thing for our nation is also doing the right thing from a personal perspective. Just as hiring my neighbor to paint my house would put money into his hands, which might contribute to upkeep on his house and, therefore, stabilize property values in the neighborhood, or be spent on goods from my company or to support other local businesses that feed into that same cycle, doing right by America has the same impact, on a much broader scale. What goes around comes around.

Initially, it may seem like a smart move to save your company a penny or two per unit produced by closing the factory and contracting with a manufacturer in China or elsewhere. But think more long-range: That wealth will be transferred abroad, thus breaking the virtuous circle. Those workers who took pride in making your company's products will now be on the street, perhaps for a year or more; their skills no longer wanted, they will begin to rust, and they will be lucky to eventually get a job making a fraction of what they used to. The wealth that used to pass through them will no longer flow into your community, and the businesses where they used to spend it will be the poorer for it. Your company may have saved 2 cents, but it also helped to undermine not just loyal employees, but those who would otherwise have provided a ready market for your products.

CONSTANT IMPROVEMENT

The pursuit of excellence is a driving force for many American workers, be they employees, managers, or entrepreneurs. For me, improving my business means pursuing excellence in everything we do. I see that excellence every day, in the thousands of products we carry on MadeinUSAForever.com and in the American manufacturers that create them. Most of these are small, family-owned businesses that know their employees personally. You can tell by chatting with them that they believe they are doing something really special and important. Whether it is a towel, pillow, shirt, or pair of jeans they are producing, they are proud to put their name on it. You can sense their passion, and see in their craftsmanship that, to them, what they do is more an art than a job. They are striving for excellence in their own way, much as I am. There is no way they would outsource to Asia, as long as they have breath left in their bodies. These are the suppliers I have the honor of working with. So deep is their commitment to what they produce that most of the owners of the small companies we work with at MadeinUSAForever.com probably would rather be out on the factory floor making the items they sell than stuck in the office, dealing with administrative tasks.

The pursuit of excellence goes hand in hand with making it in the USA. Creating something special takes heart; it cannot be contracted out to save a few pennies. Meaningless junk can be made anywhere. Workers with that heart cannot be bought or sold; they must be nurtured for years by ethical and equally hard-working managers who share their passion.

WHAT CAN COMPANIES DO?

Make your company a great American company. Be part of the solution, not part of the problem. Help the USA recover from these trying economic times, then go beyond to ensure its future and the future of our great nation.

Make money by offering true value, not by selling chintzy imports. Put your own customers to work by buying from American suppliers that build here. Stand fast in the face of future challenges to our nation. Make sure your company's employees, customers, and neighbors know that by supporting America, they will be sending a powerful message. Those who hear that message will be rewarded, as we as a nation come to recognize that our long-term interests rest here, with our own businesses and employees, and act accordingly.

This we can do, and much more. In each decision we make and then act upon, we can either add value to our nation or take it away. Making these choices is not so hard when seen in that light. Whether we work at a large corporation with thousands of employees, or are entrepreneurs working alone out of our garages, we share a common goal: to succeed for ourselves and for our nation. Through this effort, one person, one company, and one community at a time, and with the support of government, we can turn the decay into renewal and rebuild this great country.

Stand up and join me! Let's lock arms and make a real difference for our nation!

Chapter 13 Bringing It Together
Action Steps for America

It's clear that we face a number of tough challenges, but we have the resources, the people, and the determination to rebuild America. Every faction needs to work together to be part of the solution: business, government, and especially us, the people. If we do this, we will not fail. We must not fail, for the sake of our nation and generations to come.

BUSINESS

I am not a politician, lawyer, economist, or professor. I am a businessperson and entrepreneur who loves his country. Many of you reading this are also businesspeople or entrepreneurs, or soon will be. Even if you aren't currently operating a business, read this section and consider the opportunities. There is a hole in many communities right now waiting to be filled by those passionate about putting skilled employees to work creating quality goods. You could be one of them.

Aside from my family, business is my greatest passion. I have made both a personal and financial investment in something I know is special, unique, and has a grand purpose. For me, building my business has been like creating a kind of art; I am well compensated for the sacrifices I make, like working seven days a week, emotionally if not materially. There are easier paths, I know, but for me those would be much less satisfying. Dedicated businesspeople share a common bond with others who build and create. I am proud, yet humble, to be able to work with so many entrepreneurs like you at MadeinUSAForever .com. And to those of you who have learned how to play only the money game, I invite you to join us; we need you too. We need you to direct your skills toward doing the right thing. You will be surprised not just how good it feels, but that you can still make money! It is time to do the right thing.

You know me, and you know where I am coming from. I am fortunate to have a good sense of smell for money, and this has helped me survive and prosper. I smell the opportunity to make money now. This economic downturn has been harsh and painful, but I see it also as a rare opportunity to do the right thing for our nation, and make good money, too. For example, the cost of renting or buying prime facilities is already beginning to stabilize in some places—though certainly others are still sinking. Also, tooling and machinery makers are selling their wares practically at cost, just to keep their facilities running.

As I just said, a very rare opportunity is on the horizon, with costs lower than we've seen in decades, or maybe ever! In some cities, you will be handed the keys to facilities for practically nothing, because they are so desperate to get businesses like yours in there—businesses that will make things and help turn their economies around by investing in them and employing good people. Making that stand with local government and our people will more than just make a huge difference to our country, it will be profitable for you, too. You can be a hero to one of them.

To take full advantage of this opportunity, while at the same time help our nation out of its worst crisis in nearly a century, we need to strike while the iron is hot. For example, as soon as those commercial real estate agents sense any improvement in the market, they are going to raise rents and prices back to the levels we saw 5 or 10 years ago. Locking in low costs now is the smart thing to do.

American businesses have got to get back in the game—the American game. It is just a question of when. It is time to move beyond internationalist greed. If companies want to rely on American consumers and taxpayer bailouts, particularly the national retailers, they need to look out for America first. They can no longer be little more than import agents for foreign manufacturers. They must step up and at least dedicate sections of their stores to American-made goods, similar to organic produce sections in groceries.

Any opportunity to purchase products or supplies is a potential opportunity to buy American.

Weakening of investor confidence caused by billion-dollar scams has hurt our nation as a whole. Punishment for such scams is so inconsequential that it does not serve as a true deterrent. Businesspeople shown to have defrauded customers, investors, and suppliers should be made to suffer more severe punishment.

American businesses need to invest here and hire Americans; they need to have a little faith the economy will improve. They can't make it here if they don't have the equipment, factory, and workforce in place. But if they wait too long, they will lose a lot of great opportunities. The businesspeople who will profit the most from America's resurgence will be those who make the investment early and help resurrect this country, with an eye toward long-term profits and a renewed economy.

Making an investment here means buying the machinery necessary to make the products, and securing the facilities where they will be manufactured. Yes, it is very hard to get credit these days, but projects that show increased revenue and greater profitability are more interesting to bankers than those making desperate pleas to cover cash flow shortfalls.

If you are a business owner, manager, or executive, do this quick exercise right now: Take out a few pieces of paper or flip open your laptop and jot down some brief notes about what you could do if you were not so concerned about conserving cash. This is a form of brainstorming, so there is no wrong answer. Draft three plans of what you would do with various amounts of capital—say, $10,000 for a smaller business (like mine), or $100,000, $1 million, $10 million, whatever is appropriate for your business—and what that could do for your company's revenue and profitability. Don't let any negative thoughts seep in just now; your goal is to just float some positive ideas.

For example, maybe you could produce 10,000 more units a month if you were to purchase those three new machines you have been wanting. That would let you finally move that outdated machine to the swing shift (when every machine and person is running to meet demand). With the added volume spread across fixed costs, and a bit more efficiency, perhaps you could squeeze $0.20 greater margin per unit throughout the plant. Those added units would then bring $1 more in margin per unit. If you could take the whole plant to 50,000 units a month, including those 10,000 added units, it would add $20,000 in profit per month. Those three new machines cost $100,000 each, so you could pay for them in just 15 months ($300,000 total for the three machines divided by $20,000). Thereafter, all that new cash flow is free and clear. That would give you the production capability you are going to need in busy times, as well as the margin buffer to deal with the bad times. And with the new machinery, you will be able to go toe-to-toe with those chintzy Chinese imports and finally push them back into the sea.

Positive cash flow from day one and a payoff in 15 months? Heck, even that banker down the street has got to like those numbers! Plus, it shows you are taking smart steps to grow to that next level, to make your firm both stronger and more agile.

Now take this info and enter it onto a spreadsheet or a couple PowerPoint presentation sheets, then grab the brochures from the machinery supplier and go down and talk to that banker. Proactive businesspeople get attention at the bank. Whiners find they cannot get any more credit.

Surprise! By brainstorming for just a few minutes, you have allowed the ideas that probably have already been brewing in your head to gel into an action plan for growing (or maybe even saving) your company. I know you, because you and I are very much alike; and I know you have probably been conserving cash just as I was. Now it is time to go for it.

Businesspeople who take advantage of this period in time to get really good deals on equipment and facilities will find they are in a position of strength when the economy does turn around. Imagine the head start you will have over those who waited to expand until the economy was firmly back on track! They will have to pay top dollar for equipment and facilities, whereas your cost advantage will be pretty much permanent. Luck? You make your own luck, and one way to do that is to stand with America now, not later.

Now let's do a similar exercise for your employees. Grab another piece of paper and write down the type and caliber of the next three full- or part-time employees you would like to hire. What work would you get off your own desk right this second if you could? Where could production be that much more efficient? Is the back office obviously suffering from lack of help? Treat this exercise as a serious opportunity to help your organization, and the country, too.

For the moment, don't worry about the economy or the news coming out of Washington. Just focus on that list. Based on your present and future needs, and depending on the size of your business, you might even want to expand the number to 10 or even 20 people. It costs nothing to write them down. Once you have, rank them in terms of urgency.

As an entrepreneur, I know that the thought of hiring new people can be very stressful; but I relieve that stress by thinking of being able to delegate more work, freeing me to focus on more important issues—like writing this book! For example, I delayed for months before hiring a part-time person to add new product listings to MadeinUSAForever.com. After all, I thought, I can do it myself for free. Right? Wrong. That logic works only if you have spare time. I realized there are only seven days in a week, and time was slipping away from me; and I was getting more and more behind by doing something I could easily hand off to a qualified, eager, and, frankly, inexpensive employee. The weight it took off my shoulders was amazing; at the same time, I felt good that I was able to give someone a real job, thereby adding real value.

Here is a message for you, creative entrepreneur: Make yourself much more efficient. Do what you love to do, and do best, and hire others to do the things that you don't enjoy, or that don't require your personal attention, or that someone else might do even better. Some people enjoy routine tasks, or are gifted at detail-oriented tasks, or just want a steady paycheck and a job that doesn't spill over into their private lives. I was amazed to find that setting aside mundane tasks unleashed my creative energy to do more important things for my business. If necessary, I can always cover those tasks, or train another new person.

Furthermore, much as real estate and equipment costs have been dropping rapidly of late, the cost of hiring new people has gone through the floor. A lady who saw my truck (with MadeinUSAForever.com painted on it) in the parking lot of a supermarket realized I must either employ folks or know those who do. She ran up with her resume in hand and offered to start at $10 per hour. Others still need to have their expectations reset, however. A dad came by to pitch his son to work for me. His son, he told me, is involved in cycling and could only work two days a week; but he wanted $10 an hour in spite of having no experience. A nice guy, but I had to wonder what universe he was living in. In general, though, the marketplace is full of hard-working, highly qualified, and innovative people who now have much lower pay expectations in this economy. Do I feel bad paying them less than they were making at their former jobs? Considering that I did not pay myself at all during the first three years I was building MadeinUSAForever.com, the answer is no. However, as entrepreneurs, we have to understand that if we want to keep good employees, they will need to be rewarded as they grow.

Are you feeling more energized now to invest in America and hire people? So am I!

As businesspeople, we also need to consider training issues in local communities. We cannot realistically expect to find workers in every community with the specialized skills we need; nor can we expect the government to provide that training to meet our time frame. What we do need to do is work with government to find a longer-term solution, and accept that we're going to have to take the initiative ourselves in the short term.

To address this problem now, we need to invest in hiring and training employees ourselves to fill the roles that are opening up. Get past the fear that these people will leave as soon as they are fully qualified. If training requires a substantial investment, cover that investment with a contract. For instance, agree to pay for employees' training in full as long as they agree to stay in their jobs for five years; if they leave within the first year, you'll be entitled to 100 percent reimbursement, 80 percent in the second year, and so on. For example, let's say you spend $6,000 to send an employee out of state to train him or her, and that person quits two years later; then he or she owes you $3,600. At the same time, it is a good idea to give raises to those who go through the training and are now effectively using the skills you paid for to improve your company. This both encourages future growth and helps ensure that your workers want to remain in your employ.

To conclude this section, I want to discuss a topic about which I have received many calls from entrepreneurs who manufacture here in the USA. They are very concerned about the U.S. Chamber of Commerce. It might surprise you to hear there is a struggle within the federation. I have been told time and again that the local- and state-level chambers are great; but at the national level in Washington, it is overly concerned with the internationalist and national retail chain agenda of keeping the markets open to chintzy foreign goods, at the expense of USA-based manufacturing. For example, it is very hard to understand the chamber's opposition to efforts in the Senate to pass a bill assisting U.S.-based businesses to bring outsourced jobs back to this country.[1] I do not personally have time to get involved in this issue at this time, but I wanted to bring it to your attention. The Chamber works for all members, not just for the Wal-Marts of the world. As such, it needs to be the champion of American manufacturing at every level, not just city and state levels, if it wants to continue to play the leadership role it is paid to play. It's time to turn up the heat on this organization.

GOVERNMENT

It is *our* government, not government by and for big businesses or lobbyists. We, the citizens of the United States, own the government; not the other way around. Government must stand with the people and business to rebuild our nation.

The government is made up of lots of different people, most of whom care about America's future. The politicians aside, from my perspective, the main difference between those working in the private sector and public sector is the degree of urgency. Years ago, people went into government knowing their wages would be lower than in the private sector, but they also knew they could expect a less intense daily pace of work and good benefits, like a pension. Ironically, as wages in the private sector suffered from the decay of manufacturing, government wages began to look pretty good. Now, however, things seem to be balancing out, since the economic downturn has left many public pensions seriously underfunded. States like California, where I live now, enabled a few public employees acting like parasites to "spike" pension plan payouts. These states allowed their pension payout formulas to be manipulated by fudging vacation time and making questionable overtime allocations, leading to six-figure pensions well beyond what the public understood. Without meaningful change, California, Illinois, New York, and other states race toward bankruptcy, at which point the courts will eventually be called upon to reduce these payouts.

As angry as I am about the lack of stewardship by the leaders of our states and federal government, I realize that most of the people who work for our governments are conscientious, and mean well. And most of them are probably as upset about the condition of our government as we are. It is tempting to dismiss the government as inept and simply try to ignore what it's doing and get on with our lives; but what we really need to do is come together to turn this situation around.

The government is the biggest purchaser of goods and services here in the United States. Military spending alone has kept some industries alive in this country. Washington negotiates our treaties and trade agreements (cough, cough). It collects taxes from us. It prints our currency. It sends our men and women abroad to fight our wars. It is the ultimate backstop for the economy. And those are just a few of the many important duties the government performs, to varying degrees of success; some it does quite well, while it seriously fails at others. We must try to reorient our government's priorities toward pro-Americanism and encourage legislators to support policies that maximize good jobs here.

Government is supposed to serve its people, not the money interests. Let's consider a ban on lobbyists for 10 years and see the good that results. Take the money out of the game and let our elected officials do their jobs. Seriously: Let's think about no paid lobbying for 10 years; no former elected officials or their staffs cashing in; no big corporations or foreigners buying influence; just the voices of real, involved citizens letting legislators know what is important to them. And perhaps we should require all federally elected officials to reveal corporate and association donations on their Web sites within three business days of accepting them.

It is time for our government to do first what is right for our people. No more unbalanced treaties. No more pretending there is open free trade with Asia. Instead of negotiating treaties that close our factories, government should be strongly motivating foreign manufacturers to move their factories here. I'm not talking about just screwing a frame on a television in this country but about creating real value within the United States.

Most importantly, we need a level playing field, where China and others are now "gaming": currencies, environmental issues, worker and product safety, accountability, and patent rights. If foreign companies cannot be held liable, for whatever reason, the government of that company must accept the financial liability. Any activity that deliberately undermines our manufacturers' ability to compete, such as manipulating a currency to the point at which it is undervalued by 40 percent, must be met with automatic tax duties to level the playing field. Keep in mind, we are dealing with countries that are playing this game to win, all while Washington dozes. That must change. We must be as clever as our international trading "partners," or limit access to our markets on a much broader scale. In the same way we now treat food production and protection of family farmers as priorities, we must nurture manufacturing in this country, even if it means restricting foreign access in the same way our manufacturers are restricted from doing business abroad.

Since buying American-made products adds so much more value to our economy than purchasing imports, our tax policies should encourage production here. Value-add taxes are used in some countries along the production process; a value-add credit to help restore American manufacturing would stir a lot of interest in the business community, to keep and build factories at home. The positive economic effect would be much greater than the cost. For example, if a 3 percent value-add credit were paid for $1 of real economic value created here, the positive economic impact after the multiplier effect would be $1.70, and the cost only $0.03.

More than labeling all items with the country of origin, we also should consider placing larger labels on the front of all packaging: One that states, "Citizens of the USA were employed to make this item," for domestically produced products; and a second, in red, for imports, that states, "No citizens of the USA were employed to create this item."

We need as well to seriously review international agreements like NAFTA and the WTO to determine whether they are in our interest, and conduct annual checkups that require independent verification of the number of jobs created or lost here. Every other nation in the world approaches these agreements with an eye on the net gain or loss of jobs, and the effect on wages. They do not sign such agreements where there is a loss; neither should we. These factors in all alliances must be net zero or in our favor, or no deal. Ross Perot was right about the sucking sound, but it is not just jobs going to Mexico; it is also China, and to a much greater degree.

Duties on imports are charged against the declared wholesale value of the goods, whereas they should be charged on the full retail value of the items.

Tens of millions of toys were recalled in 2007 due to the lead paint issue and other safety concerns, and none of them were made in the USA. Our government took no action against the foreign manufacturers or the retail chains that support them. Instead, it put new burdens on the handful of toy manufacturers still here in the United States. No one is checking for dangerous chemicals at our borders and ports; meanwhile, our own government imposes additional burdens on our own manufacturers, even putting some out of business. Unlike foreign manufacturers, domestic manufacturers are held liable, and could even go to jail, if they use dangerous chemicals. Why the double standard? Why penalize on our own manufacturers but not foreign sources? If our safety were the government's primary concern, foreign imports would be subjected to the same kind of regulations that domestic manufacturers must meet. I suspect our elected officials had to show they were "doing something," at the same time lobbyists for the big retail chains were working hard to ensure that their foreign sources would not be limited. I have a good friend whose son was exposed to too much lead from one of these foreign sources, and his health will be affected the rest of his life. That lead will never flush out of his brain. Where is the outrage? Why isn't the government that is supposed to be protecting us testing all imported toys at the border and ports? Every cargo container should be opened, and at least a few of the goods in it should be checked randomly for dangerous chemicals.

Let's start at the bottom. What might a city council do for a small community if it were faced with a key plant closure? Its members would likely consider urgent efforts to attract new businesses to the community. They might offer tax incentives to woo a new manufacturer. They might even take over closed facilities and make sure they are up to code, and potentially improved, in order to give that new manufacturer a running start. They would probably also take stock of their people's skills, in concert with the unemployment situation, in order to understand the kind of firm that would be the best fit for the community. They might even consider revamping adult education programs to ensure that future employers get their workforce needs met, assuming a maker of a specific type needs special skills. In short, these council members would likely take a number of proactive steps to enable their economy to recover.

What is the difference between that community and state and federal governments? All should be orientating themselves toward maximizing overall private sector employment and wages. Basic math shows that public sector employment based on taxes or borrowing cannot rise above a certain threshold for long before it torpedoes the economy itself. To ensure a healthy economic recovery, sustainable jobs must come from the private sector. I have explained again and again how the service economy has a much smaller positive economic effect than manufacturing. The answer for the country, nearly every state, and all but a handful of communities is to have good manufacturing jobs.

The preceding example of how an individual community could prioritize local jobs should be the model for such cities as Sacramento, Springfield, Albany, and, especially, Washington in approaching meaningful job creation. Spending does not "create" a job, unless that job can exist after the money goes away, any more than growing an orchid in a greenhouse produces a flower capable of surviving the winter in Rochester, New York. Conversely, investing money in a private sector job, via a skill or initial subsidy, to snatch that job back from overseas and bring it back here is money well spent.

The government should follow the example set by that small city council, and respond appropriately to this emergency situation. Job maximization means making things here. Interestingly, the difference between the needs of the small city and the federal government are really just a matter of scale. The difference in the way they are being handled is a matter of sad irony.

Government, like business, should be evaluating safe maximization of the private sector economy in every decision it makes. In fact, given that the government exists to represent the people, its focus should be even more intent than that of private industry. Let's reach out to government at all levels to stand with us and help make our nation great again.

PEOPLE

Millions of people are actively concerned about U.S. job creation, and tens of millions more are sympathetic. That is a good start, but we need much greater involvement if we are really to turn this situation around. The momentum is growing every day, but we require more than just sympathy; we need people who are willing to take an active part in this effort. We need tens of millions of people standing together, with business and government, to make the renewal of America a reality.

The average American has to wake up and realize that rebuilding this great nation really matters to them, to their family's financial health and employment. Whether or not they have a job, whether it is in business or government, they need to remember that only a healthy economy can pay for those jobs.

The critical question is how to take this movement beyond those who are already active on these issues to the majority, who are either unaware or too apathetic to act. We need many millions more if we are to move beyond occasional label checking and to a real commitment to buy American-made, whenever and wherever possible, and to support government initiatives to bring good manufacturing jobs back to this country.

The starting point for action is the big retail chain stores. They are the main gateways through which imports enter our lives, and they are susceptible to consumer pressure. If enough customers demand American-made products, they will make room for them, in the same way many grocers have done for organic food products. That's a start—a foot in the door. But we must push the door wide open. Once these chains have proof that many customers are willing to pay a premium for higher-quality, longer-lasting USA-made products, they will expand offerings of those products. But we must continue to exert pressure. Those of us who genuinely care about this issue have a special duty to spread the word to others, and it's one we can feel really good about.

To reiterate what I said in Chapter 8, in a polite, friendly way, reach out to everyone you know. Start with those who are already sympathetic to the cause but who may not be actively thinking about this topic when buying new items. Encourage them to reach out to others. Think of all the people you know, and the many others they know, and so on. We each have a lot more influence than we realize. We each have an opinion that others value and respect. That you care about this issue will go a long way toward winning others over, beyond the many good reasons for just doing it. With tens of millions of Americans aligning with business and government, we can make our nation great again.

We all know certain people who seem to "know everybody," and to be sources of information for a wide audience; some of them have more influence than others. These are the people who tend to be trend setters within their extended circles of friends and acquaintances. They collect and share information, and often have a much wider circle of influence than the average person; they network in numerous ways: verbally, through e-mail, blogs, Facebook, LinkedIn, Twitter, online forums, social clubs, volunteer organizations, and many other outlets. Getting through to these trendsetters is an excellent way to get our message out to a much broader audience, for they are among those who can shape public opinion. If they say a new restaurant is a must, or that you really must see this movie, people in their circle tend to take their advice and act on it. Their opinions seem to take on a life of their own, and so they can help spread our message widely and rapidly.

If each of us takes the time to reach out to just one person every day, and then even a fraction of them do the same, the thousands will become hundreds of thousands, then millions.

One of the greatest things for me about founding MadeinUSA Forever.com was discovering the amazing diversity of those who are passionate about this issue and want to see positive change. This is not a red-state versus a blue-state issue; it is a red, white, and blue issue, one that affects all Americans. Join with me to renew America and make her strong again, to ensure good jobs for ourselves and our kids, and a healthy future.

This issue can unify us, rather than divide us, unlike others that politicians argue over to maintain their power. It can bring us together as a people, no matter what our background, creed, or color. Issues that divide us do little more than energize different segments of our population against one another to illicit an emotional response to donate, vote, or both. Unifying issues, in contrast, bind us and our culture together, and can heal not just the wounds of economic decay, but social issues, too. Having enough good jobs solves a lot of important problems, most obviously unemployment among our young people, giving them a stake in our nation's future. A growing economy would pay for our schools while helping to pay down the national debt. An America that once again supports factories is also one that can defend itself and spread freedom around the world. All of this and more we can accomplish in a few short years if we just do one simple thing: Buy American-made.

Because this issue is unifying, it is useful, even fun to reach out to others. Simply by saying, "You know I am worried about America's future, since we don't make much here anymore," you lay a common ground on which nearly anyone, from progressive to conservative can stand. From this point, it is energizing to realize how much we really all do have in common, though we may not agree at all on certain "hot potato" issues. Millions of U.S. citizens who are passionate about buying American will find that, no matter what their background, they share something truly important: a belief in the renewal of this great country.

Reaching out to local media, to newspapers and radio stations, is another way to generate surprisingly good results. Very often, thoughtfully expressed and carefully written letters to the editor will get printed in local papers, especially on a fresh topic. A follow-up call to the editor in charge of the relevant section of the paper will further increase the odds it will be published. Even if your letter isn't published, the editor may give you some good advice for rewording it so that it will be at a later date; you may even plant a seed that will lead to a full-blown article in the paper.

With all of us, together with business and government, standing together, arms locked, we can rebuild this country, heal its wounds, create good-paying jobs by the millions, and rise again like a phoenix. When we stand together, we can find solutions to almost any problem. We find hope instead of despair. See light instead of dark. Choose action over apathy.

Together, we can make it a reality. Stand with me.

Conclusion   Be a Hero

One thing I have learned over the years is how short life really is, and how little time we have to find meaning and make a real difference. In old age, we look back and ask, "Did I accomplish my goals, or at least give it a fighting try? Did I do something worthwhile or just limp along between television episodes?"

It seems to me that the sum of our lives is in what we learned, what we believed, what we acted on, whether we made things better, whether we stood for justice, and whether we loved well and long.

Suffering and darkness are growing in our great nation, but it does not have to be that way. We know now that our decline is tied directly to the short-term greed that encourages our factories to close. We know what those low, low prices are actually costing us, our children, the environment, and the people of other countries. We know now, and so now we must act. Believing in justice does nothing for our future, our children's futures, or our country's future if we continue to act immorally or even unthinkingly. With knowledge comes responsibility. That may be a heavy burden now, but it will be nothing compared to the weight of looking back years from now and realizing that when we had solutions within reach, and the chance to implement them, we did nothing.

The myths and lies are fading, like the morning mist, leaving us a choice between two difficult routes: helping our nation to heal and reach new heights, or watching it fade into history. One requires hard work and sacrifice for years to come; the other allows for a few more years of ignoring the truth, followed by enforced sacrifice caused by years of decay and financial ruin. Will future generations remember us as the one that stood up to the tough challenges, or the one that went down for the count?

These are the lies they tell us, or that we unwittingly repeat to ourselves, so that we feel okay about getting through the day: Talk of service jobs replacing manufacturing jobs is a painful lie, as our own government data shows. Another is that global "free trade" is real; I witnessed during my years living in Asia that trade is only free heading into the United States. Our government also ignores the safety concerns associated with products coming from these nations, particularly, China; and we must face the difficult fact that we have no legal recourse. Tens of millions of toys recalled in 2007, and still our government does nothing to test products crossing our borders.

The tales of King Arthur so many of us enjoyed in our youth bear a resemblance to early European myths in which the hero pulls the magic sword out of a stone, tree, or other hard place and then brings order to chaos. It seems to me that the sword could also symbolize the knowledge the hero gains as he grows beyond the adventures of youth to shoulder the burden of wisdom after seeing the bigger picture. Ignorance may be bliss, but it makes one incapable of changing things for the better. It is knowledge, together with wisdom, that eventually allows the hero to triumph.

What is worth taking a stand for in life? Our families, our way of life, freedom and country, among other important things. What if all of these were ultimately wrapped up in the same defining moment? That moment is approaching.

Standing for our nation and beliefs and for our ability to manufacture are one and the same. We can no longer call ourselves a superpower if we cannot even supply, much less pay for, our troops. We cannot have sufficient good-paying jobs if we don't have factories that provide good manufacturing jobs. We cannot pay for local or federal government because the taxes those factories would pay if they stayed here are being shipped abroad.

As I write these words, I am sitting in the shade at a park. A father with three young boys just jumped out of a Chevy pickup truck, and the boys ran off to play. What, I wondered, will those boys be doing for a living in 10 or 20 years? Will they have a better quality of life, or even the same quality their folks enjoyed? What are their dreams? It is for our children, grandchildren, and generations of Americans yet unborn that we must make this stand.

Perhaps, for these boys, their father is their hero. If we each picked a hero from our past or present, or even from fiction, what would that hero do when faced with the knowledge of his or her nation's decline? Would that hero sit by and do nothing? Would he or she make an excuse like, "I am just one person," or give into apathy? No. That hero would stand and do something meaningful, to make a difference. Can you imagine John Wayne riding off in a Honda Civic into the sunset? No! Would Rosie the Riveter settle for the unemployment line? No! What would your hero do? Let me tell you a secret: *You* are that hero, in so many ways. Not just to yourself, but to those around you.

My heroes include the men and women in our armed services, fighting for our nation and freedom across the globe. With our manufacturing base shrinking so those chain stores can get the low, low pricing they seek (read: Wal-Mart), what hope do these heroes have to find good jobs after they return from making so many sacrifices for our country? At least after World War II, the Korean War, and even the Vietnam War, our soldiers had a reasonable chance of getting decent work when they came home. It is now for the sake of heroes returning from places like Iraq and Afghanistan that we have to take a stand.

Every small difference that each one of us makes creates a ripple effect: helping someone who in turn helps others. Imagine that multiplied by thousands, tens of thousands, and, eventually, millions. Everything we buy was made somewhere. With every one of the purchase decisions we make we are either helping our own people or we are helping someone else—often, a crooked politician or factory owner totally unconcerned with the welfare of his or her employees and customers. Buying an article of American-made clothing benefits more than just the person who made it; your choice benefits an entire chain of people, from the farmer who grew the cotton through every step of the process, until it reaches your hands. All those people are working because of you. When more of us commit to buying American-made, we help those people to keep the faith, put food on their tables, and buy other products that were also made by Americans.

We can be brave and choose action, or we can close our eyes to what's happening as our nation sinks into oblivion.

One thing I learned living in Asia is that although our nation is not perfect, it is unique in that it stands for the best humankind has to offer. That has been true since our forefathers landed on this continent and began to build a new kind of society. World history gives us some reasons to hope; sadly, however, it is dominated by stories of countries shifting between tyranny and chaos. Throughout the uncounted volumes of history books I have read, force is nearly always the defining factor. There was only one country that tore off those chains of tyranny and made something new: the United States of America.

The light of freedom and liberty shining from this land has attracted millions from all over the world determined to have better lives; more, it has inspired hundreds of millions around the globe to see past the dark lessons of history and throw off the shackles that bound them.

This inspiring light in the darkness is, however, fragile. Every generation must nurture and protect it against the most insidious enemy of liberty and freedom: apathy. One generation of Americans beat the Great Depression, Nazi Germany, and Imperial Japan. Another stood off Communism. However, at our height of power, the cancers of apathy and short-term greed had already started spreading, just when our abundance seemed as if it would last forever. People in this country stopped caring about where things were being made, just as they stopped caring about our nation's health. It does not have to be that way. For each of us who takes a firm stand, 10 more will notice, and many of them will find the courage to join us. Ten more will notice each of those people, and soon we will become a powerful movement.

If we really care about our environment, it is very important to understand the facts. Products made in the USA must meet certain pollution emission requirements; likewise, their transport to their final destinations is strictly regulated. All vehicles must meet pollution standards. One of the main cost advantages of making items in countries like China is the near complete lack of enforced regulation of pollutants spewing into the air and water, making those items anything but "green." And it gets worse from there. Recall what I explained earlier about those huge cargo container ships: They are a major cause of global pollution. They use "bunker" fuel, which contains 2,000 times the level of sulfur and other pollutants. That dirty oil they burn equates to pollution emissions from 50 million cars for one year.

Reading about this shocking amount of pollution caused me to wonder how much is emitted just to bring a single Toyota or Hyundai to the USA. Here is my estimate: First, let's assume, generously, that those ships are actually twice as efficient, at 25 million "car years" (the amount of pollution an average car produces in one year) of pollutants spewed out annually. The transport ships in service generally carry about 6,500 cars and can, assuming very fast unloading, make about 26 round trips annually between Yokoyama, Japan, or Pusan, South Korea, and Long Beach, California, and return to Asia almost empty. One round trip would release pollutants amounting to about 1 million car years; therefore, dividing that number by the load of 6,500 car years would give us the number of car years of pollution generated: 153 car years of pollution produced to bring just one car over from Asia! That is not green, not at all! In contrast, a domestically produced car, because it has to be transported according to our country's strict pollution control laws, would result in vastly less pollution moving that car from the factory to the car dealer. Clearly, that is the green choice; and the same goes for any import versus domestically produced product. No matter the scale, because those cargo container ships are unregulated for most of their trips across the Pacific, the green choice is always going to mean domestically produced.

Similar appalling levels of pollution are expelled by those giant oil tankers that bring all that foreign oil here, which is yet another crucial reason we must break our addiction to foreign oil.

The petroleum deficit is draining between $20 and $30 billion from our economy every month; but we can stop the leak. By closing the energy trade gap, we can recapture wealth currently being depleted from the United States, as well as help to protect the freedoms so many energy-supply nations do not support, and cut off the flow—however indirect—of our money to terrorist organizations hostile to this country. Once we have developed our own sources of energy and learned to use them more efficiently, we will never again feel compelled to send our troops into enemy territory and sacrifice American lives simply to protect our oil supply.

Let's hit the energy deficit head-on. In the immediate term, increasing efficiency and reducing consumption is the quickest route to achieve this goal; it also is, by far, the best bang for the buck. At the same time, we can get a start on the medium-term effort to upgrade our energy production and distribution capabilities. And, finally, looking longer term, we must invest in, invent, develop, and bring to useful fruition, alternative energy technologies here in the United States.

As I mentioned in Chapter 3, though the energy deficit is a daunting challenge, it is more easily solvable than the goods import deficit, through moderate behavioral change and doing what Americans do best, innovating. We have the tools, the creativity, the ability, and the reason. What we need right now is the leadership and a heightened sense of urgency to beat the energy deficit.

By now, you know a lot about why I quit my executive-level job in the technology industry to found MadeinUSAForever.com. I put my passion, resources, energy, and abilities to the test in order to provide an alternative to what the big chain stores expect us to accept blindly. I was making a lot of money as I climbed the corporate ladder, but could not ignore the growing realization of what was really going on in Asia, and what it meant to our nation and our children's future. Living and working in Asia twice, when I had unprecedented access to the business centers in those nations, was a revelation. I went over there fully believing the "free trade is good at any cost" lie and others I heard in college and in corporate life. With my love of history and learning, I could hardly resist the opportunity to live in Asia and, more, to get beyond the typical experiences of most foreigners there. Issues like pollution, worker safety conditions at subcontractors, and China's ardent drive to be the world's next superpower, through manufacturing, had me second-guessing all I'd learned previously. The realization of what the extensive hollowing out of U.S. industry meant for our great nation's future and my young children's future haunted me after I returned to this country. Instead of being an internationalist, getting richer while my country was growing poorer,

I decided I would use all my resources and knowledge to help turn the situation around. It has been amazing, and empowering, to watch MadeinUSAForever.com grow, to be able to help new American suppliers and meet so many awesome customers. I have never looked back. Instead, I'm looking forward to the next surge forward, to the moment when it becomes apparent to those large retailers that we, as Americans, have remembered who we are, what we care about, and how to effect change in our world.

Are you with me? Will you stand with me to restore jobs, retool our nation, and compete with the world? To see the USA re-made?

Please think about what you have read in this book and the many ideas that may have occurred to you while going through it. It's easy to become outraged and then motivated while reading a book or watching a documentary and then, all too quickly, let that feeling slip away as we get on with our lives. But we cannot afford to lose motivation now. I can promise you it feels great to be part of the solution—even a small one. What can you do to help in your way? Whom can you talk to? What can you do differently? The beauty of being a free American is that you have a thousand options; and now that you understand the situation, you can make your own decisions about how to best use your particular skills, talents, passions, and connections to turn the tide.

Those big retailers believe they have a special power because of their traditional role in the American shopping experience. They want us to be little more than consumer drones, who do not challenge what they sell us. We owe it to ourselves to prove them wrong. We can badger them until they give in, starting by devoting sections in their stores to "Made in USA" products. It will grow from that modest start.

As long we continue to pressure—peacefully—the chain stores and Washington, we will gain, and be able to hold, the moral upper ground. We must make both the retailers and Washington realize that we the people hold the real power.

Standing together we will make change happen! Good jobs will return. Manufacturing will be restored. We will be able to compete on equal footing with any country in the world. The USA will be re-made!

Thank you for reading this book and for being a part of the solution in the movement to renew our great nation!

God bless the United States of America!

Notes

INTRODUCTION

1. Sun Tzu, *The Art of War*, trans. Lionel Giles (1910), Chapter 3, paragraph 18, www.chinapage.com/sunzi-e.html (accessed August 10, 2010).

CHAPTER 1

1. United States Merchant Marine, "Liberty Ships," www.usmm.org/libertyships.html (accessed September 8, 2010).
2. "Health Risks of Shipping Pollution Have Been Underestimated," *The Guardian*, April 9, 2009, www.guardian.co.uk/environment/2009/apr/09/shipping-pollution.
3. David M. Kennedy, *Freedom from Fear: The American People in Depression and War, 1929–1945* (New York: Oxford University Press, 1999), 543.
4. Bureau of Economic Analysis, "U.S. International Transaction Accounts Data," www.bea.gov/international/index.htm#trade (last modified June 16, 2010).
5. Centers for Disease Control and Prevention, "Drywall Information Center," www.cpsc.gov/info/drywall/index.html (accessed April 3, 2010).
6. U.S. Department of State, "2008 Human Rights Report: Vietnam," www.state.gov/g/drl/rls/hrrpt/2008/eap/119063.htm (last modified February 29, 2009).
7. Boeing, "B-52 History," www.boeing.com/history/boeing/b52.html (accessed September 18, 2010).

CHAPTER 2

1. Central Intelligence Agency, *The World Fact Book*, www.cia.gov/library/publications/the-world-factbook/geos/ks.html (accessed September 19, 2010).

2. "China's Holdings of U.S. Securities: Implications to U.S. Economy," Congressional Research Service Report for Congress, January 8, 2008, p. 3, http://fpc.state.gov/documents/organization/99496.pdf.

3. Central Intelligence Agency, *The World Fact Book*, www.cia.gov/library/publications/the-world-factbook/geos/ja.html (accessed September 19, 2010).

4. "China's Holdings of U.S. Securities: Implications to U.S. Economy," Congressional Research Service Report for Congress, July 30, 2009, p. 3, www.fas.org/sgp/crs/row/RL34314.pdf (accessed September 14, 2010).

5. Ibid.

6. Cnn.com, "U.S. Death Toll from Korean War Revised Downward," June 4, 2000, http://archives.cnn.com/2000/US/06/04/korea.deaths (accessed September 12, 2010).

CHAPTER 3

1. U.S. Census Bureau, "Comparison of Real and Nominal Oil Imports," www.census.gov/foreign-trade/statistics/graphs/PetroleumImports.html (accessed September 18, 2010).

2. American Lawn Mowers, "About Us," www.reelin.com/AboutUs.aspx (accessed September 12, 2010).

CHAPTER 4

1. U.S. Bureau of Labor Statistics, "Civilian Workers, by Major Occupational and Industry Group," www.bls.gov/news.release/ecec.t01.htm (last modified September 8, 2010).

2. "More People Get Real Estate Licenses," *San Francisco Business Times*, May 25, 2007, www.bizjournals.com/eastbay/stories/2007/05/28/story3.html.

CHAPTER 5

1. *The Wall Street Journal Online*, www.wsj.com (accessed September 13, 2010).

2. United States Postal Service, "Statement of Postmaster General," December 2, 2010, www.usps.com/communications/newsroom/testimony/2010/pr10_pdonahoe1202.htm.

CHAPTER 6

1. *New World Encyclopedia*, "Han Chinese," www.newworldencyclopedia.org/entry/Han_Chinese (accessed September 16, 2010).

2. *Encyclopaedia Britannica*, "The Great Wall of China," www.britannica
   .com/EBchecked/topic/243863/Great-Wall-of-China (accessed September
   16, 2010).
3. *Encyclopaedia Britannica*, "Manchu," www.britannica.com/EBchecked/
   topic/361411/Manchu (accessed September 16, 2010).
4. *New World Encyclopedia*, "Manchukou," www.newworldencyclopedia
   .org/entry/Manchukuo (accessed September 16, 2010).
5. *Encyclopaedia Britannica*, "Taiwan History," www.britannica.com/
   EBchecked/topic/580902/Taiwan (accessed September 16, 2010).
6. LivePhysics.com, "China's First Atomic Bomb 1964," www.livephysics
   .com/physics-videos/history/china-first-atomic-bomb-1964.html
   (accessed September 16, 2010).
7. UN General Assembly, Fifty-fourth Session, Resolution 2758, www.un
   .org/ga/54/agenda/a194.pdf (accessed September 10, 2010).
8. PBS's *American Experience: The Presidents*, "Richard M. Nixon,"
   www.pbs.org/wgbh/amex/presidents/37_nixon/nixon_domestic.html
   (accessed August, 8, 2010).
9. "Deng Xiaoping," *People's Daily Online*, http://english.peopledaily
   .com.cn/data/people/dengxiaoping.shtml (accessed August 16, 2010).
10. Sun Tzu, *The Art of War*, trans. Lionel Giles (1910), Chapter 3, para-
    graph 2, www.chinapage.com/sunzi-e.html (accessed August 10, 2010).

CHAPTER 7

1. *The Wall Street Journal Online*, www.wsj.com (accessed September 14,
   2010).
2. Bryan Rich, "The Most Undervalued Currency in the World," *Money
   and Markets,* October 31, 2009, www.moneyandmarkets.com/the-
   most-undervalued-currency-in-the-world-4-36242.

CHAPTER 8

1. *Entrepreneur.com*, "Sam Walton: Bargain Basement Billionaire,"
   October 9, 2008, www.entrepreneur.com/growyourbusiness/radical-
   sandvisionaries/article197560.html.
2. Lands' End, "Gary Comer," www.landsend.com/aboutus/company_
   info/index.html (accessed September 17, 2009).

CHAPTER 9

1. *DoingBusiness.com*, "Starting a Business," www.doingbusiness.org/
   ExploreTopics/StartingBusiness (accessed September 21, 2010).

2. SBA.gov, "Frequently Asked Questions," www.sba.gov/advo/stats/sbfaq.pdf (accessed September 21, 2010).

3. "Health Risks of Shipping Pollution Have Been Underestimated," *The Guardian*, April 9, 2009, www.guardian.co.uk/environment/2009/apr/09/shipping-pollution.

4. *The Times Higher Education*, "The Top 200 Universities," www.timeshighereducation.co.uk/world-university-rankings/2010–2011/top-200.html#score_OS|sort_country|reverse_false (accessed September, 25, 2010).

CHAPTER 10

1. David Halberstam, *The Reckoning* (New York: Avon Books, 1986).

CHAPTER 12

1. U.S. Bureau of Labor Statistics, "Civilian Workers, by Major Occupational and Industry Group," www.bls.gov/news.release/ecec.t01.htm (last modified September 8, 2010).

CHAPTER 13

1. Jay Heflin, "U.S. Chamber Comes Out Against Senate Outsourcing Bill," *The Hill*, September 23, 2010, http://thehill.com/blogs/on-the-money/domestic-taxes/120667-us-chamber-comes-out-against-senate-outsourcing-bill (accessed September 24, 2010).

Acknowledgments

One of the most intelligent people I have ever met, Tiffany Sanders, has been very helpful in making this book readable and, frankly, better. As long as there are people like her, our society has reason to hope.

Thank you to Robert Hall, for assisting to collect that important data. In real life, he is a bard, and I know his song "Dollar to the Giant" will be a big hit.

Thanks also to the many thousands of customers and hundreds of family-owned suppliers who make MadeinUSAForever.com possible. Because you stand with us, together, we are making a real difference for our nation.

Most of all, I want to thank my wife and kids for being so supportive and patient during these grueling months, when the business and this book took up all my days and nights. How to explain what Daddy is doing to a four- and two-year-old? Perhaps someday they will read these words and know that I love them, and that the sacrifice was so that they and other kids could have a chance to know the USA where I grew up—where even the sky is no limit.

Index